Copyright© 2006 by Landauer Corporation
Projects Copyright© 2006 by Lynette Jensen

This book was produced and published by
Landauer Books
A division of Landauer Corporation
3100 NW 101st Street, Urbandale, IA 50322
800/557-2144; www.landauercorp.com

President: Jeramy Lanigan Landauer
Editor-in-Chief: Becky Johnston
Cover Design: Laurel Albright
Creative Director: Lynette Jensen
Photographer: Keith Evenson
Technical Writer: Sue Bahr
Technical Illustrators: Lisa Kirchoff

We also wish to thank the support staff of the
Thimbleberries® Design Studio:
Sherry Husske, Virginia Brodd, Renae Ashwill,
Ardelle Paulson, Kathy Lobeck, Clarine Howe;
Julie Jergens, Leone Rusch, and Julie Borg.

The following manufacturers are
licensed to sell Thimbleberries® products:
Thimbleberries® Rugs (Colonial Mills);
Thimbleberries® Quilt Stencils
(Quilting Creations); and Thimbleberries®
Sewing Thread (Robison-Anton Textile
Company).

All rights reserved. No part of this book may be
reproduced or transmitted in any form by any
means, electronic or mechanical, including
photocopying, recording, or by any information
storage and retrieval system without permission
in writing from the publisher, except as noted.
The publisher presents the information in this
book in good faith. No warranty is given, nor are
results guaranteed.

Library of Congress Cataloging-in-Publication
Data available on request.

This book printed on acid-free paper.
Printed in China

10-9-8-7-6-5-4-3-2-1

ISBN 10:   0-9770166-8-4
ISBN 13: 978-0-9770166-8-6

CONTENTS

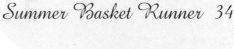
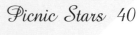

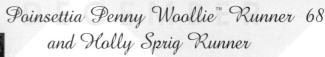

Winter Scape

January

Winter Scape

20 x 26-inches

Fabrics and Supplies

1/4 yard **DARK BLUE PRINT** for star background

6 x 42-inch **GOLD PRINT** for stars and pieced border

4 x 42-inch piece **GOLD FLORAL** for stars

3 x 42-inch piece **GREEN PRINT #1** for trees

3 x 42-inch piece **GREEN PRINT #2** for trees

1/8 yard **BEIGE PRINT #1** for tree background

1/4 yard **MEDIUM BLUE PRINT** for snowman background

1/8 yard **RED DIAGONAL PRINT** for inner border

1/8 yard **RED PRINT** for pieced border

3/8 yard **LARGE PINE PRINT** for outer border

9-inch square **BEIGE PRINT #2** for snowman appliqués

1/3 yard **RED PRINT** for binding

2/3 yard backing fabric

paper-backed fusible web for appliqué

tear-away fabric stabilizer (optional)

No. 8 pearl cotton for decorative stitches: black

quilt batting, at least 24 x 30-inches

Before beginning this project, read through
Getting Started on page 77.

Star Section

Cutting

From **DARK BLUE PRINT**:

- Cut 2, 1-1/2 x 42-inch strips.
  From the strips cut:
  2, 1-1/2 x 4-1/2-inch rectangles
  12, 1-1/2 x 2-1/2-inch rectangles
  12, 1-1/2-inch squares
- Cut 4, 1-7/8-inch squares

From **GOLD FLORAL**:

- Cut 1, 2-1/2 x 42-inch strip.
  From the strip cut:
  1, 2-1/2-inch square
  4, 1-7/8-inch squares
  8, 1-1/2-inch squares

From **GOLD PRINT**:

- Cut 1, 1-1/2 x 42-inch strip.
  From the strip cut:
  12, 1-1/2-inch squares

Piecing

Step 1 Position a 1-1/2-inch **GOLD FLORAL** square on the right edge of a 1-1/2 x 2-1/2-inch **DARK BLUE** rectangle. Draw a diagonal line on the square and stitch on the line. Trim the seam allowance to 1/4-inch; press. Make 8 units. Sew a 1-1/2-inch **DARK BLUE** square to the right edge of each unit and press. At this point each unit should measure 1-1/2 x 3-1/2-inches.

Make 8

Step 2 With right sides together, layer the 1-7/8-inch **DARK BLUE** and **GOLD FLORAL** squares together in pairs. Press together, but do not sew. Cut the layered squares in half diagonally to make 8 sets of triangles. Stitch 1/4-inch from the diagonal edge of each pair of triangles and press.

Make 8, 1-1/2-inch triangle-pieced squares

Step 3 Sew triangle-pieced squares to both side edges of each 1-1/2-inch **GOLD PRINT** square; press. At this point each unit should measure 1-1/2 x 3-1/2-inches.

Make 4

Step 4 Sew the Step 1 units to the top and bottom edges of the Step 3 units and press. At this point each star block should measure 3-1/2-inches square. Referring to the Step 7 diagram, sew the star blocks together in pairs; press.

Make 4

Step 5 Position a 1-1/2-inch **GOLD PRINT** square on the corner of a 1-1/2 x 2-1/2-inch **DARK BLUE** rectangle. Draw a diagonal line on the square; stitch, trim, and press. Repeat this process at the opposite corner of the rectangle.

Make 4 star point units

Step 6 Sew star point units to the top and bottom edges of the 2-1/2-inch **GOLD FLORAL** square; press. Sew 1-1/2-inch **DARK BLUE** squares to both side edges of the remaining star point units; press. Sew the units to the side edges of the **GOLD FLORAL** square; press. Sew 1-1/2 x 4-1/2-inch **DARK BLUE** rectangles to the top and bottom edges of the star block; press. At this point the star block should measure 4-1/2 x 6-1/2-inches.

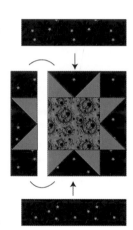

Make 1

Step 7 Sew the Step 4 star block units to both side edges of the Step 6 star block; press. At this point the star section should measure 6-1/2 x 10-1/2-inches.

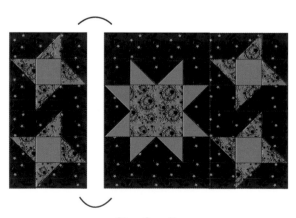

Star Section
Make 1

Tree/Background Section

Cutting

From **GREEN PRINT #1**:

- Cut 1, 1-1/2 x 42-inch strip. From the strip cut:
  - 6, 1-1/2 x 4-1/2-inch rectangles
  - 2, 1-1/2 x 2-1/2-inch rectangles

From **GREEN PRINT #2**:

- Cut 1, 1-1/2 x 42-inch strip. From the strip cut:
  - 2, 1-1/2 x 4-1/2-inch rectangles
  - 2, 1-1/2 x 3-1/2-inch rectangles

From **BEIGE PRINT #1**:

- Cut 2, 1-1/2 x 42-inch strips. From the strips cut:
  - 2, 1-1/2 x 7-1/2-inch rectangles
  - 2, 1-1/2 x 4-1/2-inch rectangles
  - 4, 1-1/2 x 2-1/2-inch rectangles
  - 4, 1-1/2 x 2-inch rectangles
  - 12, 1-1/2-inch squares

From **MEDIUM BLUE PRINT**:

- Cut 1, 5-1/2 x 42-inch strip. From the strip cut:
  - 2, 5-1/2 x 8-1/2-inch rectangles

Piecing

Step 1 Position a 1-1/2 x 2-1/2-inch **BEIGE #1** rectangle on the corner of a 1-1/2 x 2-1/2-inch **GREEN #1** rectangle. Draw a diagonal line on the **BEIGE #1** rectangle; stitch, trim, and press. Repeat this process at the opposite corner of the **GREEN #1** rectangle. At this point each unit should measure 1-1/2 x 4-1/2-inches.

Make 2

Step 2 Position 1-1/2 x 2-inch **BEIGE #1** rectangles on the corners of a 1-1/2 x 3-1/2-inch **GREEN #2** rectangle. Draw a diagonal line on the **BEIGE #1** rectangles; stitch, trim, and press. At this point each unit should measure 1-1/2 x 4-1/2-inches.

Make 2

Step 3 Position 1-1/2-inch **BEIGE #1** squares on the corners of a 1-1/2 x 4-1/2-inch **GREEN #1** rectangle. Draw a diagonal line on the squares; stitch, trim, and press.

Make 4

Step 4 Position a 1-1/2-inch **BEIGE #1** square on the left corner of a 1-1/2 x 4-1/2-inch **GREEN #1** rectangle. Draw a diagonal line on the square; stitch, trim, and press. Make 2 units. Repeat this process using a 1-1/2-inch **BEIGE #1** square and a 1-1/2 x 4-1/2-inch **GREEN #2** rectangle. Make 2 units.

Make 2

Make 2

Step 5 Sew the Step 1, 2, 3, and 4 units together; press. Make 2 tree units. Sew a 1-1/2 x 4-1/2-inch **BEIGE #1** rectangle to the bottom edge of each tree unit; press. Sew a 1-1/2 x 7-1/2-inch **BEIGE #1** rectangle to the right edge of each tree unit; press. At this point each tree block should measure 5-1/2 x 7-1/2-inches.

Make 2

Step 6 Position a 5-1/2 x 8-1/2-inch **MEDIUM BLUE** rectangle on the bottom corner of each tree block. Draw a diagonal line on the **MEDIUM BLUE** rectangles; stitch, trim, and press. Sew the two blocks together; press. At this point the tree/background section should measure 10-1/2-inches square.

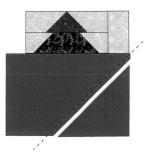 

Tree/Background Section
Make 1

Step 7 Sew the Tree/Background Section to the bottom edge of the Star Section; press. _At this point the quilt center should measure 10-1/2 x 16-1/2-inches._

Borders

Note: _The yardage given allows for the border strips to be cut on the crosswise grain. Diagonally piece the strips as needed, referring to **Diagonal Piecing** instructions on page 80. Read through **Border** instructions on page 79 for general instructions on adding borders._

Cutting

From **RED DIAGONAL PRINT**:
- Cut 2, 1-1/2 x 42-inch inner border strips

From **RED PRINT**:
- Cut 2, 1-1/2 x 42-inch strips.
  From the strips cut:
  2, 1-1/2 x 12-1/2-inch rectangles
  2, 1-1/2 x 6-1/2-inch rectangles
  4, 1-1/2 x 4-1/2-inch rectangles
  4, 1-1/2 x 3-1/2-inch rectangles

From **GOLD PRINT**:
- Cut 1, 1-1/2 x 42-inch strip. From the strip cut:
  20, 1-1/2-inch squares

From **LARGE PINE PRINT**:
- Cut 3, 3-1/2 x 42-inch outer border strips

Piecing

Step 1 Attach the 1-1/2-inch wide **RED DIAGONAL PRINT** inner border strips.

Step 2 Referring to the diagrams, position 1-1/2-inch **GOLD PRINT** squares on the corners of a 1-1/2 x 4-1/2-inch **RED PRINT** rectangle. Draw a diagonal line on the squares; stitch, trim, and press. Make 4 units. Repeat this process using the 1-1/2 x 6-1/2-inch **RED PRINT** rectangles and the 1-1/2 x 12-1/2-inch **RED PRINT** rectangles.

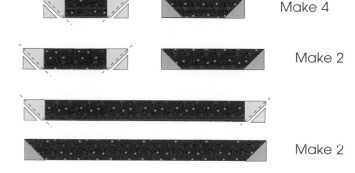

Make 4

Make 2

Make 2

Make 2

Step 3 Position a 1-1/2-inch **GOLD PRINT** square on the right corner of a 1-1/2 x 3-1/2-inch **RED PRINT** rectangle. Draw a diagonal line on the square; stitch, trim, and press.

Make 2

Step 4 Position a 1-1/2-inch **GOLD PRINT** square on the left corner of a 1-1/2 x 3-1/2-inch **RED PRINT** rectangle. Draw a diagonal line on the square; stitch, trim, and press.

Make 2

Step 5 Sew a Step 3 unit to the left edge of a Step 2, 1-1/2 x 6-1/2-inch unit; press. Sew a Step 4 unit to the right edge of this unit; press. _At this point the pieced border strip should measure 1-1/2 x 12-1/2-inches._ Make 2 pieced border strips. Sew the pieced border strips to the top and bottom edges of the quilt center; press.

Make 2

Step 6 Referring to the quilt diagram, sew 2 of the Step 2, 1-1/2 x 4-1/2-inch units to both side edges of a Step 2, 1-1/2 x 12-1/2-inch unit; press. _At this point the pieced border strip should measure 1-1/2 x 20-1/2-inches._ Make 2 pieced border strips. Sew the pieced border strips to the side edges of the quilt center; press.

Step 7 Attach the 3-1/2-inch wide **LARGE PINE PRINT** outer border strips.

Appliqué - Fusible Web Method

Step 1 Position the fusible web, paper side up, over the appliqué shapes on page 9. With a pencil, trace the shapes onto fusible web leaving a small margin between each shape. Cut the shapes apart.

*Note: When you are fusing a large shape, like the snowman, fuse just the outer edges of the shape so that it will not look stiff when finished. To do this, draw a line about 3/8-inch inside the snowman, and cut away the fusible web on this line. See **General Instructions** on page 78 for a generic diagram of this technique. Shapes will vary depending on the quilt design.*

Step 2 Following the manufacturer's instructions, fuse the shapes to the wrong side of the fabric chosen for the appliqués. Let the fabric cool and cut along the traced line. Peel away the paper backing from the fusible web.

Step 3 Referring to the quilt diagram, position the shapes on the quilt, fuse in place.

Note: We suggest pinning a rectangle of tear-away stabilizer to the backside of the quilt top so that it will lay flat when the appliqué is complete. We use the extra-lightweight Easy Tear™ sheets as a stabilizer.

Step 4 Using black pearl cotton, blanket stitch around the snowman shapes. Using 2 strands of pearl cotton make French knots for the eyes and buttons. Using 2 strands of pearl cotton stitch the mouth with the running stitch and the arms with the outline/stem stitch.

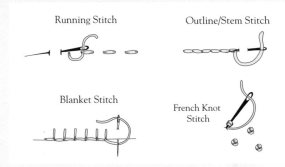

Running Stitch   Outline/Stem Stitch

Blanket Stitch   French Knot Stitch

Note: To prevent the hand blanket stitches from "rolling off" the edges of the appliqué shapes, take an extra backstitch in the same place as you made the blanket stitch, going around the outer curves, corners, and points. For straight edges, taking a backstitch every inch is enough.

Putting It All Together

Trim the backing and batting so they are 4-inches larger than the quilt top. Refer to **Finishing the Quilt** on page 80 for complete instructions.

Binding

Cutting

From **RED PRINT:**
• Cut 3, 2-3/4 x 42-inch strips

Sew the binding to the quilt using a 3/8-inch seam allowance. This measurement will produce a 1/2-inch wide finished double binding. Refer to **Binding** and **Diagonal Piecing** on page 80 for complete instructions.

Winter Scape
20 x 26-inches

Quilting Suggestions

Winter Scape Snowmen

Large Snowman
Trace 1 onto
fusible web

Medium Snowman
Trace 1 onto
fusible web

Small Snowman
Trace 1 onto
fusible web

Patchwork Heart
Tablecloth

February

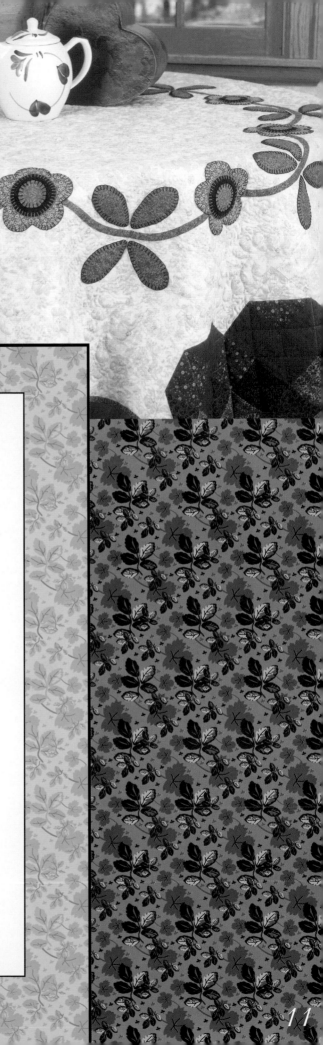

*P*atchwork *H*eart Tablecloth

58-inches square

Fabrics and Supplies

6 x 42-inch piece *each* of **7 ASSORTED RED PRINTS**
for heart blocks

2-3/8 yards **BEIGE FLORAL** for center square and borders

3/8 yard **LIGHT RED PRINT** for flower appliqués

1/8 yard **BLACK PRINT** for outer flower center appliqués

1/8 yard **GOLD PRINT** for inner flower center appliqués

3/4 yard **GREEN PRINT** for vine and leaf appliqués

5/8 yard **GOLD PRINT** for binding

3-3/4 yards backing fabric

quilt batting, at least 62-inches square

paper-backed fusible web

template material

tear-away fabric stabilizer (optional)

pearl cotton or machine embroidery thread

for decorative stitches: black, gold

**Before beginning this project, read through
Getting Started on page 77.**

Heart Units

Cutting

From **ASSORTED RED PRINTS**:
* Cut a total of 8, 3-7/8-inch squares
* Cut a total of 68, 3-1/2-inch squares

From **BEIGE FLORAL**:
* Cut 1, 3-7/8 x 42-inch strip. From the strip cut:
   8, 3-7/8-inch squares

Piecing

Step 1 With right sides together, layer the 3-7/8-inch **ASSORTED RED** and **BEIGE FLORAL** squares. Press together, but do not sew. Cut the squares in half diagonally to make 16 sets of triangles. Stitch 1/4-inch from the diagonal edge of each pair of triangles; press. <u>At this point each triangle-pieced square should measure 3-1/2-inches square.</u>

     Make 16, 3-1/2-inch triangle-pieced squares

Step 2 Sew 2 of the triangle-pieced squares to both side edges of a 3-1/2-inch **RED** square; press. Make 8 units. Sew together 3 of the 3-1/2-inch **RED** squares; press. Make 8 units. Sew the units together in pairs; press. <u>At this point each unit should measure 6-1/2 x 9-1/2-inches.</u>

Make 8
Make 8

Make 8

Step 3 Sew together 3 of the 3-1/2-inch **RED** squares; press. Make 12 units. Sew the units together to make 4 squares. <u>At this point each unit should measure 9-1/2-inches square.</u>

Make 12

Make 4

Step 4 Sew together 4 of the Step 2 units and 4 of the Step 3 units in pairs; press. <u>At this point each unit should measure 9-1/2 x 15-1/2-inches.</u>

Make 4

Quilt Center

Cutting

From **BEIGE FLORAL**:
* Cut 1, 40-1/2-inch center square
* Cut 4, 9-1/2 x 42-inch strips. From the strips cut:
   4, 9-1/2 x 28-1/2-inch border strips

Quilt Center Assembly

Step 1 Sew Step 2 heart units to the side edges of 2 of the 9-1/2 x 28-1/2-inch **BEIGE FLORAL** border strips; press. Sew the border strips to the top/bottom edges of the 40-1/2-inch **BEIGE FLORAL** center square; press.

Make 2

Step 2 Referring to the quilt diagram, sew Step 4 heart units to the side edges of the remaining 9-1/2 x 28-1/2-inch **BEIGE FLORAL** border strips; press. Sew the border strips to the side edges of the center square unit; press. <u>At this point the quilt top should measure 58-1/2-inches square.</u>

Appliqué

Cutting

From **GREEN PRINT**:
* Cut 8, 1-3/8 x 13-inch **bias** strips.
   Diagonally piece the strips together to get the length needed.

Prepare the Vines

Fold each 1-3/8-inch wide **GREEN** strip in half lengthwise with wrong sides together; press. To keep the raw edges aligned, stitch a scant 1/4-inch away from the edges. Fold the strip in half again so the raw edges are hidden by the first folded edge; press. Hand-baste if needed. Set the vine strips aside.

Fusible Web Appliqué

Step 1 Position the fusible web, paper side up, over the appliqué shapes on page 14. With a pencil, trace the shapes onto fusible web the number of times indicated on the pattern pieces, leaving a small margin between each shape. Cut the shapes apart.

Step 2 Following the manufacturer's instructions, fuse the shapes to the wrong side of the fabric chosen for the appliqués. Let the fabric cool and cut along the traced line. Peel away the paper backing from the fusible web.

Step 3 Referring to the quilt diagram, position the prepared vines and shapes on the quilt top; pin in place. Using matching thread, hand or machine appliqué the vines in place. Fuse the remaining shapes in place.

Note: We suggest pinning a rectangle of tear-away stabilizer to the backside of the quilt top so that it will lay flat when the appliqué is complete. We use the extra-lightweight Easy Tear™ sheets as a stabilizer. When the appliqué is complete, tear-away the stabilizer.

Step 4 We hand blanket stitched around the shapes using pearl cotton. If you like you could machine blanket stitch around the shapes using Mettler® embroidery thread for the top thread and regular sewing thread in the bobbin.

Blanket Stitch

Note: To prevent the hand blanket stitches from "rolling off" the edges of the appliqué shapes, take an extra backstitch in the same place as you made the blanket stitch, going around the outer curves, corners, and points. For straight edges, taking a backstitch every inch is enough.

Putting It All Together

Cut the 3-3/4 yard length of backing fabric in half crosswise to make 2, 1-7/8 yard lengths. Refer to **Finishing the Quilt** on page 80 for complete instructions.

Binding

Cutting

From **GOLD PRINT**:
• Cut 6, 2-3/4 x 42-inch strips

Sew the binding to the quilt using a 3/8-inch seam allowance. This measurement will produce a 1/2-inch wide finished double binding. Refer to **Binding** and **Diagonal Piecing** on page 80 for complete instructions.

**Patchwork Heart Tablecloth
58-inches square**

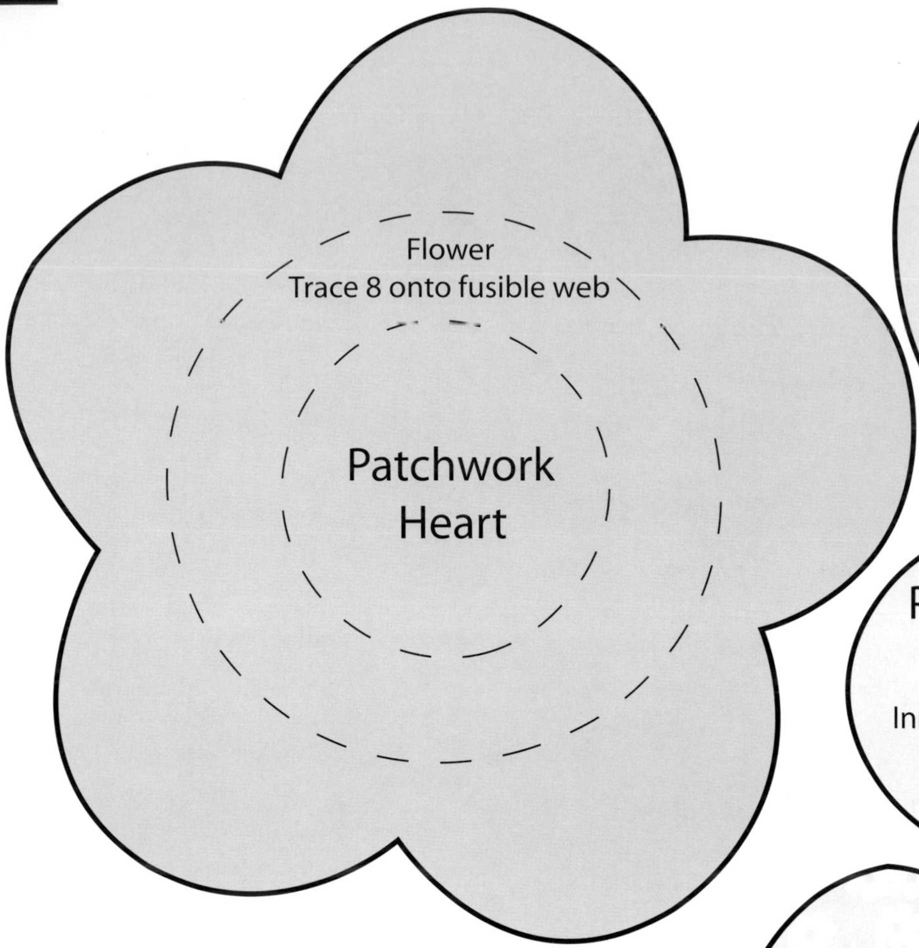

Flower
Trace 8 onto fusible web

Patchwork Heart

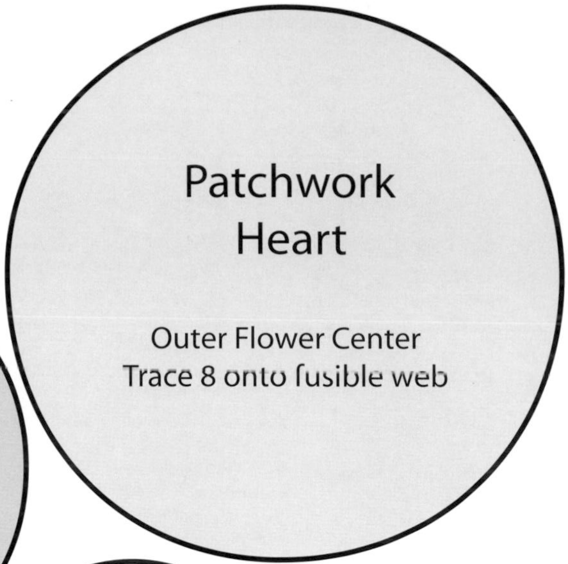

Patchwork Heart

Outer Flower Center
Trace 8 onto fusible web

Patchwork Heart

Inner Flower Center
Trace 8 onto fusible web

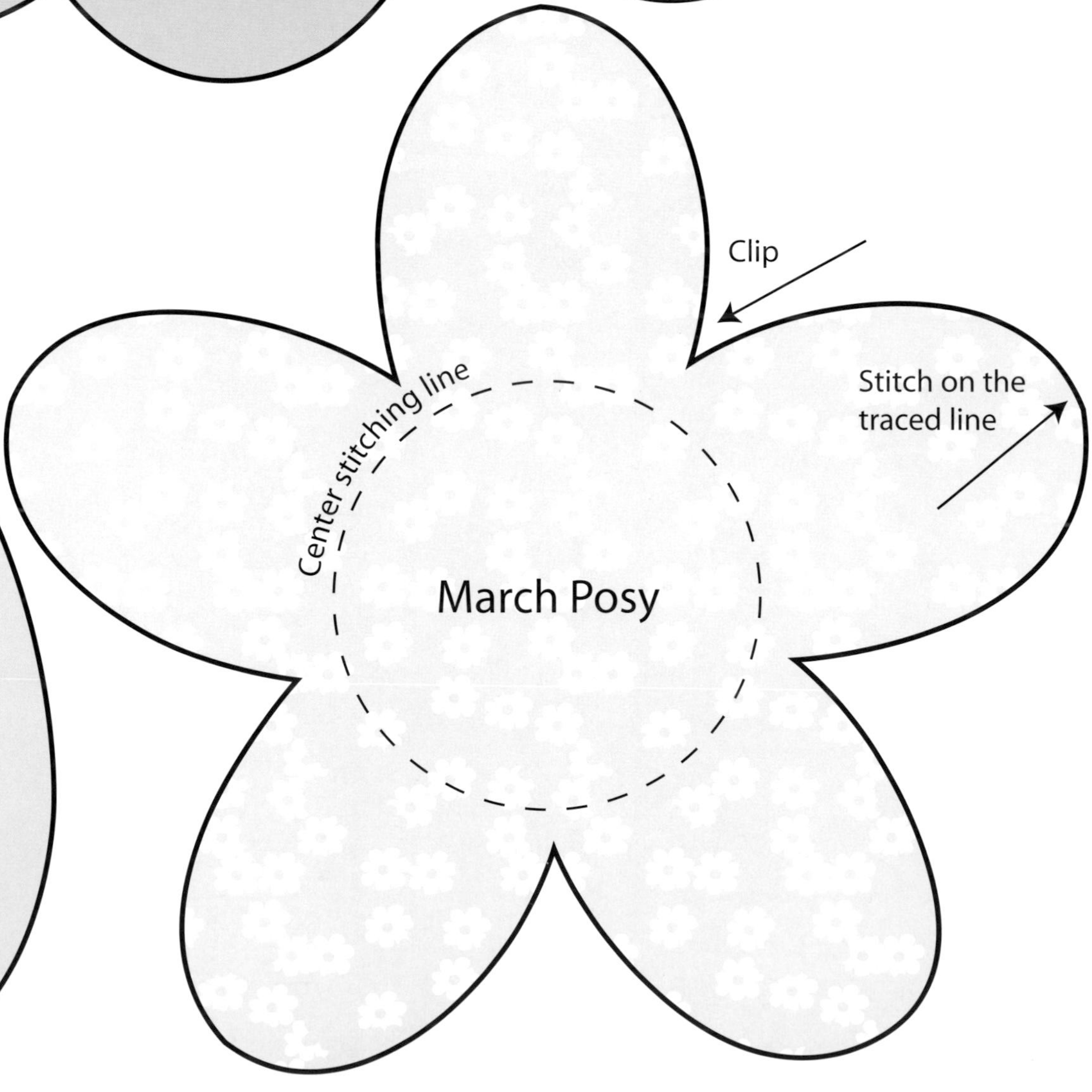

Clip

Stitch on the traced line

Center stitching line

March Posy

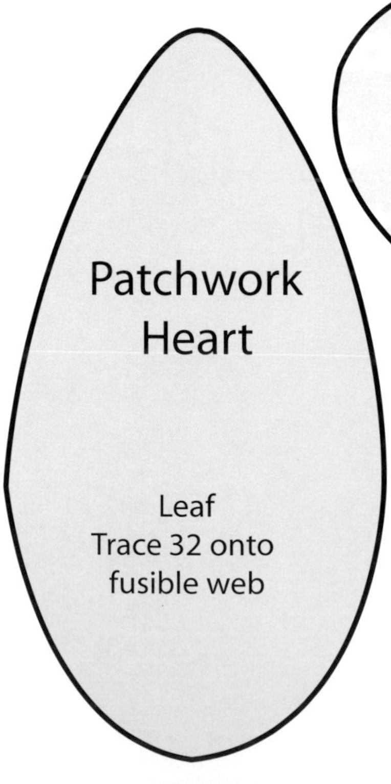

Patchwork Heart

Leaf
Trace 32 onto fusible web

March Posy

 Layer 2, 6-1/2-inch Print squares with right sides together.

 Trace the March Posy flower shape on page 14 onto the wrong side of 1 of the squares. Stitch the squares together on the traced line using a small stitch length.

 Trim the seam allowance to 1/8-inch; clip the corners being careful not to clip through the stitching line.

 Mark a 2-1/4-inch circle on the back side of the flower. Carefully cut a slit in the back piece.

 Turn the flower right side out; press. Stitching on the marked circle, make running stitches through both layers using quilting thread.

 Pull up the stitches, gathering the flower base to the back side of the flower; securely knot the thread.

 Sew a button in the center of the flower. Wrap the flower base with florist tape. Wrap the flower base to the stem wire.

Star Table Square

March

Star Table Square

45-inches square

Fabrics and Supplies

3/8 yard **GOLD PRINT** for star block

1/3 yard **GOLD FLORAL** for star block

1/2 yard **BEIGE PRINT #1** star block

1/2 yard **BLUE PRINT** for dogtooth border
and corner squares

3/8 yard **BEIGE PRINT #2** for dogtooth border

1/2 yard **GREEN PRINT** for inner border
and corner squares

7/8 yard **BROWN FLORAL** for outer border

5/8 yard **BLUE PLAID** for binding (cut on the bias)

3 yards backing fabric

quilt batting, at least 49-inches square

Before beginning this project, read through
Getting Started on page 77.

Star Block

Cutting

From GOLD PRINT:

- Cut 1, 6-7/8 x 42-inch strip. From the strip cut:
  2, 6-7/8-inch squares. Cut the squares
  diagonally in half to make 4 large
  triangles.
  4, 3-7/8-inch squares. Cut the squares
  diagonally in half to make 8 small
  triangles.
- Cut 1, 3-7/8 x 42-inch strip

From GOLD FLORAL:

- Cut 1, 3-7/8 x 42-inch strip
- Cut 1 more 3-7/8 x 42-inch strip.
  From the strip cut:
  8, 3-7/8-inch squares. Cut the squares
  diagonally in half to make 16 small
  triangles.

From BEIGE PRINT #1:

- Cut 1, 6-7/8 x 42-inch strip. From the strip cut:
  4, 6-7/8-inch squares. Cut the squares
  diagonally in half to make 8 large
  triangles.
- Cut 1, 6-1/2 x 42-inch strip. From the strip cut:
  4, 6-1/2-inch squares

Piecing

Step 1 With right sides together, layer the
3-7/8 x 42-inch **GOLD PRINT** and **GOLD FLORAL**
strips. Press together, but do not sew. Cut the
layered strips into squares. Cut the squares in half
diagonally to make 12 sets of triangles. Stitch
1/4-inch from the diagonal edge of each pair of
triangles; press. <u>At this point each triangle-pieced
square should measure 3-1/2-inches square.</u>

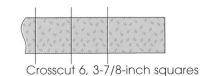

Crosscut 6, 3-7/8-inch squares

Make 12, 3-1/2-inch
triangle-pieced squares

Step 2 To make the star center units, sew a small
GOLD FLORAL triangle to the top edge of a
triangle-pieced square; press. Sew another small
GOLD FLORAL triangle to the right edge of the unit;
press. Sew a large **GOLD PRINT** triangle to the unit;
press. <u>At this point each star center unit should
measure 6-1/2-inches square.</u>

Make 4   Make 4
for star center

Step 3 Referring to the quilt diagram, sew the
Step 2 star center units together to make the star
center; press. <u>At this point the star center should
measure 12-1/2-inches square.</u>

Step 4 To make 4 of the star point units, sew a
small **GOLD FLORAL** triangle to the top edge of a
triangle-pieced square; press. Sew another small
GOLD FLORAL triangle to the right edge of the unit;
press. Sew a large **BEIGE #1** triangle to the unit;
press. <u>At this point each star point unit should
measure 6-1/2-inches square.</u>

Make 4   Make 4
for star point units

Step 5 To make 4 of the star point units, sew a
small **GOLD PRINT** triangle to the top edge of a
triangle-pieced square; press. Sew another small
GOLD PRINT triangle to the right edge of the unit;
press. Sew a large **BEIGE #1** triangle to the unit;
press. <u>At this point each star point unit should
measure 6-1/2-inches square.</u>

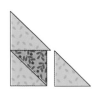

Make 4   Make 4
for star point units

Step 6 Sew the Step 4 and Step 5 star point units together in pairs; press. Make 4 star point sections. Referring to the quilt diagram, sew 2 of the star point sections to the top/bottom edges of the star center unit; press. Sew 6-1/2-inch **BEIGE #1** squares to the side edges of the remaining star point sections; press. Sew the star point units to the side edges of the star center unit; press. At this point the star block should measure 24-1/2-inches.

Make 4
for star point sections

Dogtooth Border

Cutting

From **BLUE PRINT**:
• Cut 3, 3-1/2 x 42-inch strips. From the strips cut:
16, 3-1/2 x 6-1/2-inch rectangles
4, 3-1/2-inch corner squares

From **BEIGE PRINT #2**:
• Cut 3, 3-1/2 x 42-inch strips. From the strips cut:
32, 3-1/2-inch squares

Piecing

Step 1 Position a 3-1/2-inch **BEIGE #2** square on the corner of a 3-1/2 x 6-1/2-inch **BLUE** rectangle. Draw a diagonal line on the square and stitch on the line. Trim the seam allowance to 1/4-inch; press. Repeat this process at the opposite corner of the rectangle.

Make 16
dogtooth units

Step 2 For each dogtooth border strip sew together 4 of the dogtooth units; press. At this point each dogtooth border strip should measure 3-1/2 x 24-1/2-inches.

Step 3 Sew border strips to the top/bottom edges of the star block; press. Sew 3-1/2-inch **BLUE** corner squares to both ends of the remaining dogtooth border strips; press. Sew the border strips to the side edges of the star block; press.

Borders

Note: The yardage given allows for the border strips to be cut on the crosswise grain. Read through **Border** instructions on page 79 for general instructions on adding borders.

Cutting

From **GREEN PRINT**:
• Cut 1, 6-1/2 x 42-inch strip. From the strip cut:
4, 6-1/2-inch corner squares
• Cut 4, 2 x 42-inch inner border strips

From **BLUE PRINT**:
• Cut 4, 2-inch corner squares

From **BROWN FLORAL**:
• Cut 4, 6-1/2 x 42-inch outer border strips

Attaching the Borders

Step 1 Attach the 2-inch wide **GREEN** top/bottom inner border strips.

Step 2 For the side borders, measure just the quilt top including the seam allowances, but not the top/bottom borders. Cut the 2-inch wide **GREEN** side inner border strips to this length. Sew a 2-inch **BLUE** corner square to both ends of the border strips; press. Sew the border strips to the side edges of the quilt center; press.

Step 3 Attach the 6-1/2-inch wide **BROWN FLORAL** top/bottom outer border strips.

Step 4 For the side borders, measure just the quilt top including the seam allowances, but not the top/bottom borders. Cut the 6-1/2-inch wide **BROWN FLORAL** side outer border strips to this length. Sew a 6-1/2-inch **GREEN** corner square to both ends of the border strips; press. Sew the border strips to the side edges of the quilt center; press.

Putting It All Together

Cut the 3 yard length of backing fabric in half crosswise to make 2, 1-1/2 yard lengths. Refer to **Finishing the Quilt** on page 80 for complete instructions.

Binding

Cutting

From **BLUE PLAID**:

• Cut enough 2-3/4-inch wide **bias** strips to make a 190-inch long strip

Sew the binding to the quilt using a 3/8-inch seam allowance. This measurement will produce a 1/2-inch wide finished double binding. Refer to **Binding** and **Diagonal Piecing** on page 80 for complete instructions.

Star Table Square
45-inches square

Nature's Centerpiece

A large wooden bowl filled with just a few dried Annabelle hydrangea blossoms makes a dramatic, yet very easy accessory.

• Annabelle hydrangea dry naturally on the plant. Pick blossoms when they feel dry to the touch.

To dry other flowers follow these steps:

Step 1 Pick flowers at their freshest.

Step 2 For bouquets, tie stems of blossoms together and hang upside down to dry away from humidity and bright sunlight.

Step 3 For individual blossoms, spread them out and allow to dry on newspapers. For potpourri, simply drop any deadheaded blooms into the container and allow to dry and add fragrance to the mix.

Lily Runner

April

Lily Runner

17 x 34-inches

Fabrics and Supplies

2/3 yard **BEIGE PRINT** for background

10-inch square **LIGHT GREEN PRINT** for baskets

1/4 yard **MEDIUM GREEN PRINT** for leaf
and stem appliqués

1/8 yard **PURPLE PRINT** for flowers

1/8 yard **LAVENDER PRINT** for flower

1/8 yard **GOLD PRINT** for flowers

3/8 yard **LAVENDER PRINT** for binding

5/8 yard backing fabric

quilt batting, at least 21 x 38-inches

freezer paper for appliqué

template material

*Before beginning this project, read through
Getting Started on page 77.*

Basket Blocks

Makes 2 blocks

Cutting

From BEIGE PRINT:
- Cut 1, 8-7/8 x 42-inch strip.
  From the strip cut:
  1, 8-7/8-inch square. Cut the square in half diagonally to make 2 triangles.
  4, 4-1/2-inch squares
  3, 3-1/4-inch squares. Cut the squares in quarters diagonally to make 12 triangles.
  6, 2-1/2-inch squares

From LIGHT GREEN PRINT:
- Cut 1, 8-7/8-inch square. Cut the square in half diagonally to make 2 triangles.

From MEDIUM GREEN PRINT:
- Cut 2, 1-1/2 x 6-1/2-inch **bias** strips
- Cut 4, 1-1/2 x 4-1/2-inch **bias** strips

From PURPLE PRINT:
- Cut 3, 3-1/4-inch squares. Cut the squares in quarters diagonally to make 12 triangles.

From LAVENDER PRINT:
- Cut 6, 3-1/4-inch squares. Cut the squares in quarters diagonally to make 24 triangles.

From GOLD PRINT:
- Cut 1, 2-1/2 x 42-inch strip.
  From the strip cut:
  6, 2-1/2-inch squares

Piecing

Step 1 Layer a **LAVENDER** triangle on a **PURPLE** triangle. Stitch along the bias edge as shown. Press the seam allowance toward the **LAVENDER** triangle.

Bias edges

Make 12 triangle units

Step 2 Layer a **LAVENDER** triangle on a **BEIGE** triangle. Stitch along the bias edge as shown. Press the seam allowance toward the **LAVENDER** triangle.

Bias edges

Make 12 triangle units

Step 3 Sew the triangle units together in pairs; press. At this point each hourglass unit should measure 2-1/2-inches square.

Make 12 hourglass units

Step 4 Referring to the diagram, sew together 2 of the hourglass units, 1 of the 2-1/2-inch **BEIGE** squares, and 1 of the 2-1/2-inch **GOLD** squares; press. At this point each flower unit should measure 4-1/2-inches square.

Make 6 flower units

Step 5 To prepare the stems, fold each 1-1/2-inch wide **MEDIUM GREEN** bias strip in half lengthwise with wrong sides together; press. To keep the raw edges aligned, stitch a scant 1/4-inch away from the edges. Fold the strip in half again so the raw edges are hidden by the first folded edge; press. Hand baste if needed.

Step 6 Referring to the stem placement diagram, position the prepared stems on each **BEIGE** triangle. The 4-1/2-inch long stem strips are positioned on either side of the 6-1/2-inch long stem strip. Hand baste the stems in place. The stems will be appliquéd after the block is sewn together and the leaves are appliquéd.

Stem Placement Diagram

4-1/4" 4-1/4"

Center

Step 7 Sew the **LIGHT GREEN** triangles to the prepared **BEIGE** triangles. Press the seam allowances toward the **LIGHT GREEN** triangles. Make 2 units. At this point each basket/stem unit should measure 8-1/2-inches square.

Step 8 Referring to the basket block diagram, on page 25, sew together the flower units, 4-1/2-inch **BEIGE** squares, and the triangle-pieced square; press. At this point each basket block should measure 12-1/2-inches square.

Freezer Paper Appliqué

With this method of hand appliqué, the freezer paper forms a base around which the appliqués are shaped.

Step 1 Make a template using the leaf shape on page 26. Use a pencil to trace the shape on the dull side of the freezer paper and cut out on the traced line.

Step 2 With a hot, dry iron, press the coated side of each freezer paper shape onto the wrong side of the fabric chosen for the appliqués. Allow at least 1/2-inch between each shape for seam allowances.

Step 3 Cut out each shape a scant 1/4-inch beyond the edge of the freezer paper pattern.

Step 4 Referring to the block diagram for placement, layer and pin the prepared leaf shapes on each block, tucking the ends under the stems. Pin the leaves in place. With your needle, turn the seam allowance over the edge of the freezer paper shape and hand appliqué the leaves in place. When there is about 3/4-inch left to appliqué, slide your needle into this opening, loosen the freezer paper from the fabric, and gently pull the freezer paper out. Finish stitching the appliqués in place.

Step 5 Hand-appliqué the stems in place.

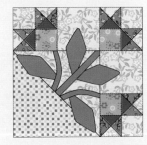

Quilt Center

Note: The side triangles are larger than necessary and will be trimmed before the binding is added.

Cutting

From **BEIGE PRINT**:
- Cut 1, 12-7/8-inch square. With a pencil, draw a line diagonally from corner to corner. Stay stitch a scant 1/4-inch on both sides of the line. Cut the square in half diagonally on the drawn line.

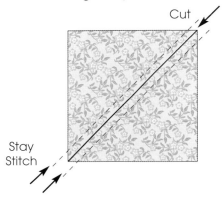

Quilt Center Assembly

Step 1 Sew together the basket blocks and side triangles in diagonal rows. Press the seam allowances toward the side triangles.

Step 2 Sew the rows together; press.

Putting It All Together

Trim the backing and batting so they are 4-inches larger than the runner top. Refer to **Finishing the Quilt** on page 80 for complete instructions.

Binding

Cutting

From **LAVENDER PRINT**:
- Cut enough 2-1/4-inch wide **bias** strips to make a 100-inch long strip

Sew the binding to the runner using a **1/4-inch seam allowance**. This measurement will produce a 1/4-inch wide finished double binding. Refer to **Binding** and **Diagonal Piecing** on page 80 for complete instructions.

Lily Runner
17 x 34-inches

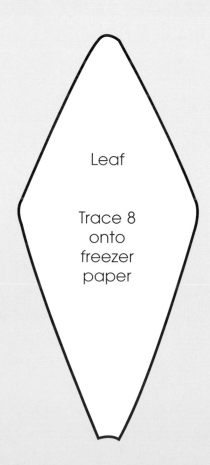

Leaf

Trace 8
onto
freezer
paper

Basket Favors

Garden peat pots transform into individual basket favors with a coat or two of paint and cutouts from floral paper napkins. Look for napkins that have small floral clusters. Coat pot with slightly diluted white glue. Place small motifs around pot pressing gently into pot. When completely dry, coat again with diluted glue. The glue will dry clear providing a nice finish. Punch holes in opposite sides of the basket and insert paper covered wire for handle. Bend 3/8-inch of each wire end up to secure.

May Basket
Place Mat

May

May Basket
Place Mat
14 x 20-inches

Fabrics and Supplies

1/2 yard **BEIGE PRINT** for place mat top

1/2 yard **GREEN DIAGONAL CHECK** for basket
appliqué and place mat back

5 x 10-inch piece **RED PRINT** for flower appliqué

5 x 10-inch piece **GREEN PRINT** for leaf appliqués

1/2 yard **GREEN PLAID** for napkin and binding
(cut on the bias)

quilt batting, at least 18 x 24-inches

template material

pearl cotton: black

1--button for flower center (1-inch diameter)

*Before beginning this project, read through
Getting Started on page 77.*

Place Mat

Cutting

From **BEIGE PRINT**:
• Cut 1, 14 x 20-inch rectangle for place mat top

From **GREEN DIAGONAL CHECK**:
• Cut 1, 18 x 24-inch rectangle for place mat back

Layer the **BEIGE** rectangle, batting, and **GREEN DIAGONAL CHECK** rectangle. Refer to **Finishing the Quilt** on page 80 for complete instructions. Quilt as desired. Trim the batting and backing even with the **BEIGE** place mat top. The place mat should measure 14 x 20-inches.

Binding

Cutting

From **GREEN PLAID**:
• Cut enough 3-5/8-inch wide **bias** strips to make an 80-inch long strip

Sew the binding to the place mat using a 1/2-inch seam allowance. This measurement will produce a 5/8-inch wide finished double binding. Refer to **Binding** and **Diagonal Piecing** on page 80 for complete instructions.

Appliqué

From **GREEN DIAGONAL CHECK**:
• Cut 2, 9 x 10-inch rectangles for basket

From **RED PRINT**:
• Cut 2, 5-inch squares for flower

From **GREEN PRINT**:
• Cut 4, 2-1/2 x 4-1/2-inch pieces for leaves

Step 1 Make templates of the basket, flower, and leaf patterns on page 31 and 32.

Step 2 Trace the basket template onto the wrong side of 1 of the **GREEN DIAGONAL CHECK** rectangles. This drawn line will be your stitching line. With right sides together, layer the 2 **GREEN DIAGONAL CHECK** rectangles; pin. Stitch the 2 layers together on the drawn line. Trim the seam allowances to 1/4-inch. Cut an X in the middle of the "basket back" piece (see diagram). Turn the basket right side out; press.

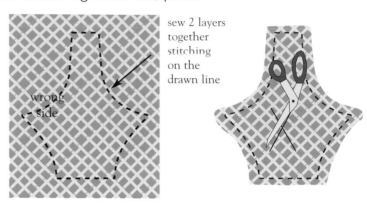

sew 2 layers together stitching on the drawn line

wrong side

Step 3 Repeat this process using the **RED** squares to make a flower. Lightly mark a 1-1/4-inch circle in the center of the flower. (When the flower and leaves are positioned on the basket this will be the stitching line to secure them all together.)

wrong side

sew 2 layers together stitching on the drawn line

lightly mark circle in center

Step 4 Using the **GREEN PRINT** rectangles, trace the leaf template onto the wrong side of 2 of the **GREEN PRINT** rectangles. With right sides together, layer the 2 rectangles on the remaining 2 **GREEN PRINT** rectangles; pin. Stitch the 2 layers together on the drawn line, leaving the straight bottom edge open for turning. Trim the seam allowances to 1/4-inch. Turn the leaves right side out; press.

wrong side

leave open

Make 2

Step 5 Referring to the diagram, layer the leaves and flower on the basket; pin. Be sure all the Xs are to the back and that the raw edges of the leaves are hidden under the flower. To secure the layers together, stitch on the center circle drawn on the flower. Sew the button in place.

Step 6 Position the basket unit on the quilted place mat. Using black pearl cotton, blanket stitch the basket unit in place along the top edge of the handle and along the sides and bottom edge.

Blanket stitch

Napkin

Cutting

From **GREEN PLAID**:
• Cut 1, 14-inch square

Stitch 1/2-inch in from the raw edges. This stitching line will determine how deep your fringe will be and it will also stop the raveling process. Using a thick needle to loosen the threads along the edges, carefully pull the threads out to make the fringe. Do not remove the threads beyond the stitching line. Tuck the napkin into the left side of the basket.

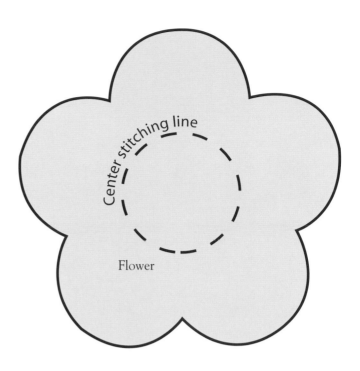

Center stitching line

Flower

May Basket Place Mat Gift Set

May Basket Place Mat

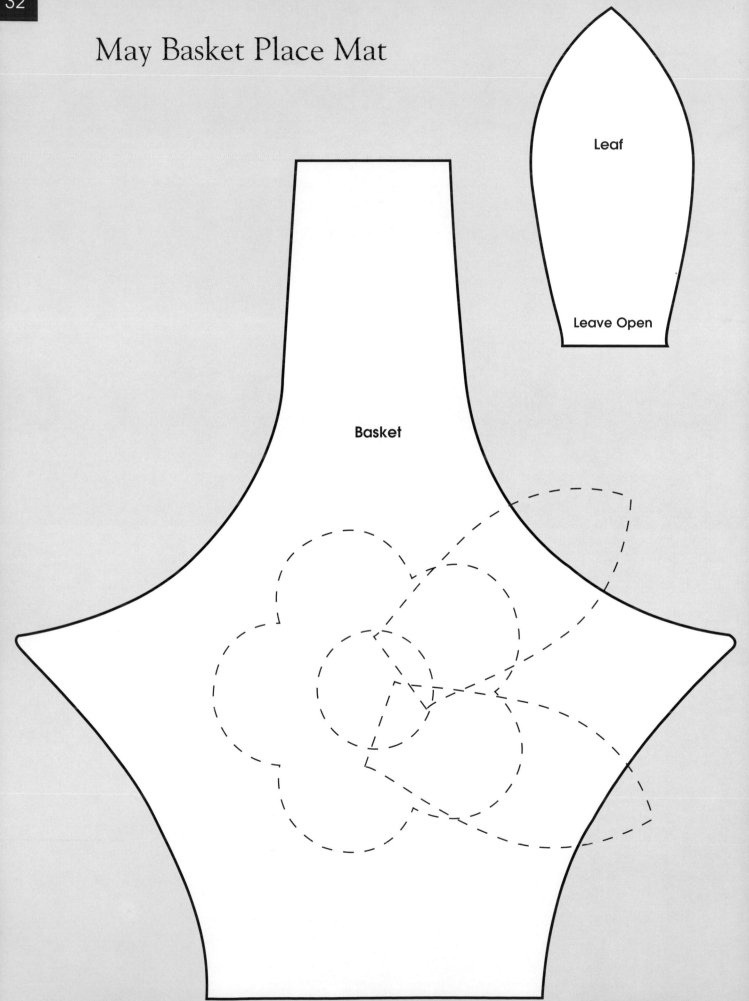

Leaf

Leave Open

Basket

Mother's Day
Recipe Gift

Use favorite recipes and vintage photographs to make a memorable Mother's Day gift. Computer generated scanned pictures work well.

Hand write recipes on special decorative papers which are available in craft and scrap booking stores. The recipes can also be typed on your computer incorporating special clip art.

Enclose the recipes in a folder made by fusing fabric to decorative paper. Cut to the desired size. Stitch a yo-yo flower to the cover. The yo-yo flower is made using a 3-1/4" circle; embellish with an antique button. Tie a waxed linen thread around the base of the flower. Wrap the thread around the folder and secure it by wrapping around the yo-yo flower.

Summer Basket Runner

June

Summer Basket Runner

19 x 37-inches

Fabrics and Supplies

1/3 yard **GREEN PRINT** for baskets

1/3 yard **DARK ROSE PRINT** for baskets and
dogtooth border

7/8 yard **LIGHT ROSE PRINT** for background
and border

3/8 yard **GREEN PLAID** for binding (cut on the bias)

2/3 yard backing fabric

quilt batting, at least 23 x 41-inches

*Before beginning this project, read through
Getting Started on page 77.*

Basket Blocks

Makes 4 blocks

Cutting

From **GREEN PRINT**:
- Cut 1, 1-1/2 x 42-inch strip. From the strip cut:
  24, 1-1/2-inch squares
- Cut 4, 1-1/2 x 11-inch **bias** strips

From **DARK ROSE PRINT**:
- Cut 1, 1-1/2 x 42-inch strip. From the strip cut:
  20, 1-1/2-inch squares

From **LIGHT ROSE PRINT**:
- Cut 1, 3-1/2 x 42-inch strip. From the strip cut:
  4, 3-1/2 x 6-1/2-inch rectangles
- Cut 2, 1-1/2 x 42-inch strips. From the strips cut:
  16, 1-1/2 x 3-inch rectangles
  8, 1-1/2 x 2-inch rectangles

Piecing

Step 1   Position a 1-1/2-inch **GREEN** square on the right corner of a 1-1/2 x 2-inch **LIGHT ROSE** rectangle. Draw a diagonal line on the square and stitch on the line. Trim the seam allowance to 1/4-inch; press. Make 4 units. Repeat this process positioning a 1-1/2-inch **GREEN** square on the left corner of a 1-1/2 x 2-inch **LIGHT ROSE** rectangle. Note the direction of the stitching line. Make 4 units.

Make 4   Make 4

Step 2 Sew a 1-1/2-inch **DARK ROSE** square to both side edges of a 1-1/2-inch **GREEN** square; press. Sew 2 of the Step 1 units to the side edges of this unit; press. <u>At this point the unit should measure 1-1/2 x 6-1/2-inches.</u>

Make 4

Step 3 Position a 1-1/2-inch **GREEN** square on the right corner of a 1-1/2 x 3-inch **LIGHT ROSE** rectangle. Draw a diagonal line on the square; stitch, trim, and press. Make 4 units. Repeat this process positioning a 1-1/2-inch **GREEN** square on the left corner of a 1-1/2 x 3-inch **LIGHT ROSE** rectangle. Note the direction of the stitching line. Make 4 units.

Make 4   Make 4

Step 4 Sew 2 of the Step 3 units to the side edges of 1 of the 1-1/2-inch **DARK ROSE** squares; press. <u>At this point the unit should measure 1-1/2 x 6-1/2-inches.</u>

   Make 4

Step 5 Position a 1-1/2-inch **DARK ROSE** square on the right corner of a 1-1/2 x 3-inch **LIGHT ROSE** rectangle. Draw a diagonal line on the square; stitch, trim, and press. Make 4 units. Repeat this process positioning a 1-1/2-inch **DARK ROSE** square on the left corner of a 1-1/2 x 3-inch **LIGHT ROSE** rectangle. Note the direction of the stitching line. Make 4 units.

Make 4   Make 4

Step 6 Sew 2 of the Step 5 units to the side edges of 1 of the 1-1/2-inch **GREEN** squares; press. <u>At this point the unit should measure 1-1/2 x 6-1/2-inches.</u>

   Make 4

Step 7 To prepare the basket handles, fold each 1-1/2 x 11-inch **GREEN** bias strip in half lengthwise with wrong sides together; press. To keep the raw edges aligned, stitch a scant 1/4-inch away from the edges. Fold the strip in half again so the raw edges are hidden by the first folded edge; press. Hand baste if needed.

Step 8 Referring to the handle placement diagram, on page 37, position the prepared handles on the 3-1/2 x 6-1/2-inch **LIGHT ROSE** rectangles and hand baste or pin in place. Machine or hand appliqué the handles in place.

Step 9 Referring to the basket block diagram, sew together the Step 2, 4, 6 and 8 units; press. <u>At this point each basket block should measure 6-1/2-inches square.</u>

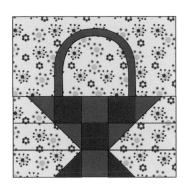

Make 4

Step 10 Sew the basket blocks together in pairs; press.

Quilt Center and Borders

*Note: The yardage given allows for the border strips to be cut on the crosswise grain. Diagonally piece the strips as needed, referring to **Diagonal Piecing** instructions on page 80. Read through **Border** instructions on page 79 for general instructions on adding borders.*

Cutting

From **LIGHT ROSE PRINT**:
- Cut 1, 12-1/2 x 42-inch strip. From the strip cut:
    1, 12-1/2 x 16-1/2-inch center rectangle
    2, 1-1/2 x 12-1/2-inch border strips
    56, 2-inch squares
- Cut 3, 2-1/2 x 42-inch outer border strips

From **DARK ROSE PRINT**:
- Cut 3, 2 x 42-inch strips. From the strips cut:
    28, 2 x 3-1/2-inch rectangles
    4, 2-inch corner squares

Quilt Center Assembly and Attaching the Borders

Step 1 Sew the basket block pairs to both short edges of the 12-1/2 x 16-1/2-inch **LIGHT ROSE** rectangle; press. Sew the 1-1/2 x 12-1/2-inch **LIGHT ROSE** border strips to the 2 short edges of the runner; press. <u>At this point the quilt center should measure 12-1/2 x 30-1/2-inches.</u>

Step 2 Position a 2-inch **LIGHT ROSE** square on the corner of a 2 x 3-1/2-inch **DARK ROSE** rectangle. Draw a diagonal line on the square; stitch, trim, and press. Repeat this process at the opposite corner of the rectangle.

Make 28 dogtooth units

Step 3 For the short dogtooth borders, sew together 4 of the dogtooth units; press. Make 2 border strips. Sew the dogtooth borders to the quilt center; press.

Step 4 For the long dogtooth borders, sew together 10 of the dogtooth units; press. Make 2 border strips. Sew 2-inch **DARK ROSE** corner squares to both ends of the border strips; press. Sew the dogtooth borders to the quilt center; press.

Step 5 Attach the 2-1/2-inch wide **LIGHT ROSE** outer border strips.

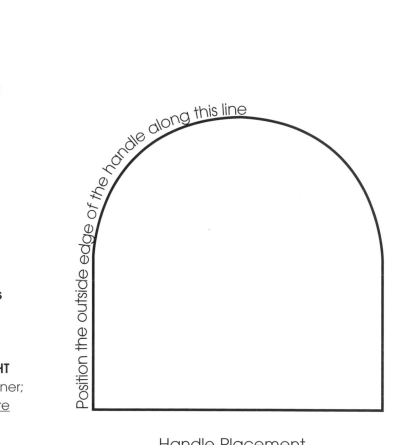

Handle Placement Diagram

Putting It All Together

Trim the backing and batting so they are 4-inches larger than the runner top. Refer to **Finishing the Quilt** on page 80 for complete instructions.

Binding

Cutting

From **GREEN PLAID**:

• Cut enough 2-3/4-inch wide **bias** strips to make a 120-inch long strip

Sew the binding to the quilt using a 3/8-inch seam allowance. This measurement will produce a 1/2-inch wide finished double binding. Refer to **Binding** and **Diagonal Piecing** on page 80 for complete instructions.

Summer Basket Runner
19 x 37-inches

Gardener's Gift Pail

Choose a pail approximately 5-inches tall and 6-inches in diameter. Cut 2 coordinating print 22-inch squares. With right sides together, sew the 2 squares together with a 1/4-inch seam allowance; leaving a 4-inch opening on 1 side for turning. Clip the corners, turn right side out; press. Hand stitch the opening closed.

Place the pail in the center of the fabric square. Pull the edges of the square up to the top edge of the pail. Use a rubber band to secure the fabric in place.

Suggestions for filling the pail: Garden gloves, seed packets, stenciled paint stick plant marker, a yo-yo flower glued onto a skewer, and other garden related gifts.

Picnic Stars

July

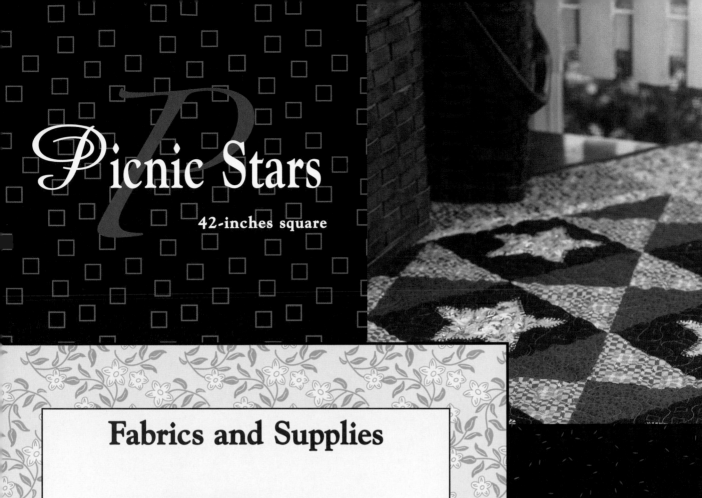

Picnic Stars

42-inches square

Fabrics and Supplies

1/2 yard **RED PRINT** for triangle blocks

1-1/8 yards **MEDIUM BLUE PRINT** for triangle blocks and outer border

1/2 yard **DARK BLUE PRINT** for appliqué foundation square

3/4 yard **GOLD PRINT** for star appliqués, inner border, and corner squares

1/2 yard **RED PRINT** for binding

2-2/3 yards backing fabric

quilt batting, at least 46-inches square

paper-backed fusible web

machine embroidery thread or pearl cotton for decorative stitches: black

tear-away fabric stabilizer (optional)

Before beginning this project, read through Getting Started on page 77.

Hourglass Blocks

Makes 13 blocks

Cutting

From **RED PRINT**:
- Cut 2, 7-1/4 x 42-inch strips. From the strips cut: 7, 7-1/4-inch squares. Cut the squares diagonally into quarters to make 28 triangles. You will be using only 26 triangles.

From **MEDIUM BLUE PRINT**:
- Cut 2, 7-1/4 x 42-inch strips. From the strips cut: 7, 7-1/4-inch squares. Cut the squares diagonally into quarters to make 28 triangles. You will be using only 26 triangles.

Piecing

Layer a **RED** triangle on a **MEDIUM BLUE** triangle. Stitch along the bias edge; press. Repeat with the remaining **RED** and **MEDIUM BLUE** triangles, stitching along the same bias edge of each triangle set. Sew the triangle units together in pairs; press. At this point each hourglass block should measure 6-1/2-inches square.

bias edges

Make 26
triangle units

Make 13
hourglass blocks

Star Appliqué Blocks

Makes 12 blocks

Cutting

From **DARK BLUE PRINT**:
- Cut 2, 6-1/2 x 42-inch strips. From the strips cut: 12, 6-1/2-inch appliqué foundation squares

Appliqué - Fusible Web Method
Step 1 Position the fusible web, paper side up, over the appliqué shapes. With a pencil, trace 12 stars onto the fusible web, leaving a small margin between each shape. Cut the shapes apart.

Note: When you are fusing a large shape, like the star, fuse just the outer edges of the shape so that it will not look stiff when finished. To do this, draw a line about 3/8-inch inside the star, and cut away the fusible web on this line. See **General Instructions** on page 78 for a generic diagram of this technique. Shapes will vary depending on the quilt design.

Step 2 Following the manufacturer's instructions, fuse the shapes to the wrong side of the fabric chosen for the appliqués. Let the fabric cool and cut along the traced line. Peel away the paper backing from the fusible web.

Step 3 Referring to the quilt diagram, position the shapes on the 6-1/2-inch **DARK BLUE** squares; fuse in place.

Note: We suggest pinning a rectangle of tear-away stabilizer to the backside of the block to be appliquéd so that it will lay flat when the appliqué is complete. We use the extra-lightweight Easy Tear™ sheets as a stabilizer. When the appliqué is complete, tear away the stabilizer.

Step 4 We machine blanket stitched around the shapes using black Mettler® embroidery thread for the top thread and regular sewing thread in the bobbin. If you like, you could hand blanket stitch around the shapes with pearl cotton.

Blanket stitch

Note: To prevent the hand blanket stitches from "rolling off" the edges of the appliqué shapes, take an extra backstitch in the same place as you made the blanket stitch, going around the outer curves, corners, and points. For straight edges, taking a backstitch every inch is enough.

Quilt Center Assembly

Step 1 Referring to the quilt diagram for block placement, sew together the hourglass blocks and the appliquéd star blocks in 5 rows of 5 blocks each. Press the seam allowances toward the star blocks.

Step 2 Sew the block rows together to make the quilt center; press. At this point the quilt center should measure 30-1/2-inches square.

Borders

Note: The yardage given allows for the border strips to be cut on the crosswise grain. Read through **Border** instructions on page 79 for general instructions on adding borders.

Cutting

From GOLD PRINT:
- Cut 1, 6-1/2 x 42-inch strip.
  From the strip cut:
  4, 6-1/2-inch corner squares
- Cut 4, 1-1/2 x 42-inch inner border
  strips

From MEDIUM BLUE PRINT:
- Cut 4, 5-1/2 x 42-inch outer border
  strips

Attaching the Borders

Step 1 Aligning long edges, sew
together the **GOLD** and **MEDIUM BLUE**
strips in pairs; press.

Step 2 Measure the quilt from left to
right through the middle to determine
the length of the border strips. Cut the
pieced border strips to this length. Sew
2 of the pieced border strips to the
top/bottom edges of the quilt center;
press.

Step 3 Sew a 6-1/2-inch **GOLD** corner
square to both ends of the remaining
pieced border strips; press. Sew the
pieced border strips to the side edges
of the quilt center; press.

Putting It All Together

Cut the 2-2/3 yard length of backing
fabric in half to make 2, 1-1/3 yard
lengths. Refer to **Finishing the Quilt** on
page 80 for complete instructions.

Binding

Cutting

From RED PRINT:
- Cut 5, 2-3/4 x 42-inch strips

Sew the binding to the quilt using
a 3/8-inch seam allowance. This
measurement will produce a 1/2-inch
wide finished double binding. Refer
to **Binding** and **Diagonal Piecing** on
page 80 for complete instructions.

Picnic Stars
42-inches square

Star
Trace 12
onto fusible web

Summertime
Prairie Point Runner

August

Summertime Prairie Point Runner

12 x 42-inches

Fabrics and Supplies

1/4 yard **ROSE PRINT #1** for flower blocks

1/4 yard **BEIGE PRINT** for flower blocks

1/8 yard **GOLD PRINT** for flower blocks

1/8 yard **GREEN PRINT** for flower blocks

3/8 yard **BLUE PRINT** for lattice/border strips

1 yard **ROSE PRINT #2** for prairie points
and facing strips

2/3 yard backing fabric

quilt batting, at least 16 x 46-inches

Before beginning this project, read through
Getting Started on page 77.

Flower Blocks

Makes 4 blocks

Cutting

From **ROSE PRINT #1**:
- Cut 2, 2-1/2 x 42-inch strips. From the strips cut:
    - 8, 2-1/2 x 4-1/2-inch rectangles
    - 8, 2-1/2-inch squares

From **BEIGE PRINT**:
- Cut 1, 4-1/2 x 42-inch strip. From the strip cut:
    - 4, 4-1/2-inch squares. Cut the squares in half diagonally to make 8 triangles.
    - 16, 1-1/2-inch squares
- Cut 1, 2-1/2 x 42-inch strip. From the strip cut:
    - 8, 2-1/2 x 4-1/2-inch rectangles

From **GOLD PRINT**:
- Cut 1, 2-1/2 x 42-inch strip. From the strip cut:
    - 8, 2-1/2-inch squares

From **GREEN PRINT**:
- Cut 1, 2-1/2 x 42-inch strip. From the strip cut:
    - 16, 2-1/2-inch squares
- Cut 1, 1-1/4 x 42-inch strip. From the strip cut:
    - 4, 1-1/4 x 7-inch stem strips

Piecing

Step 1 Position a 1-1/2-inch **BEIGE** square on the corner of a 2-1/2-inch **ROSE #1** square. Draw a diagonal line on the **BEIGE** square and stitch on the line. Trim the seam allowance to 1/4-inch; press. Make 8 units. Sew a 2-1/2-inch **GOLD** square to the left edge of each unit. Press the seam allowances toward the **GOLD** squares. Sew the units together in pairs; press. At this point each unit should measure 4-1/2-inches square.

Make 8   Make 8   Make 4

Step 2 Position a 1-1/2-inch **BEIGE** square on the upper left corner of a 2-1/2 x 4-1/2-inch **ROSE #1** rectangle. Draw a diagonal line on the square; stitch, trim, and press. Make 4 units. Position a 2-1/2-inch **GREEN** square on the right corner of each unit. Draw a diagonal line on the square;

stitch, trim, and press. At this point each unit should measure 2-1/2 x 4-1/2-inches.

Make 4

Step 3 Position a 1-1/2-inch **BEIGE** square on the lower left corner of a 2-1/2 x 4-1/2-inch **ROSE #1** rectangle. Draw a diagonal line on the square; stitch, trim, and press. Make 4 units. Position a 2-1/2-inch **GREEN** square on the right corner of each unit. Draw a diagonal line on the square; stitch, trim, and press. At this point each unit should measure 2-1/2 x 4-1/2-inches.

Make 4

Step 4 Position a 2-1/2-inch **GREEN** square on the right corner of a 2-1/2 x 4-1/2-inch **BEIGE** rectangle. Draw a diagonal line on the square, stitch, trim, and press. Make 4 units. Reverse the direction of the drawn sewing line to make another 4 units. Referring to the diagrams for placement, sew the units to the Step 2 and Step 3 units; press.

Make 4

Make 4   Make 4   Make 4

Step 5 To make a stem unit, center a **BEIGE** triangle on a 1-1/4 x 7-inch **GREEN** stem strip; stitch with a 1/4-inch seam. Center another **BEIGE** triangle on the opposite edge of the **GREEN** strip; stitch. Press the seam allowances toward the **GREEN** strip. Trim the stem unit so it measures 4-1/2-inches square.

Trim ends

Make 4
stem units

Step 6 Referring to the flower block diagram, sew together the Step 1, Step 4, and Step 5 units in rows; press. Sew the rows together to make the flower blocks; press. <u>At this point each flower block should measure 8-1/2-inches square.</u>

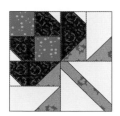

Make 4

Quilt Center and Border

Note: *The yardage given allows for the lattice/ border strips to be cut on the crosswise grain. Diagonally piece the strips as needed, referring to **Diagonal Piecing** instructions on page 80. Read through **Border** instructions on page 79 for general instructions on adding borders.*

Cutting

From **BLUE PRINT**:
* Cut 4, 2-1/2 x 42-inch strips. From the strips cut:
  2, 2-1/2 x 42-1/2-inch side border strips
  5, 2-1/2 x 8-1/2-inch lattice/border strips

Quilt Center Assembly/Attaching the Border

Step 1 Referring to the runner diagram for block placement, sew together the flower blocks and the 2-1/2 x 8-1/2-inch **BLUE** lattice/border strips; press.

Step 2 Attach the 2-1/2 x 42-1/2-inch **BLUE** side border strips.

Putting It All Together

Cut the 2/3 yard length of backing fabric in half to make 2, 21 x 24-inch rectangles. Sew the rectangles together to make a 21 x 48-inch backing rectangle. Trim the backing and batting so they are 4-inches larger than the runner top. Refer to **Finishing the Quilt** on page 80 for complete instructions.

Prairie Point Trim

Cutting

From **ROSE PRINT #2**:
* Cut 6, 4-1/2 x 42-inch strips. From the strips cut:
  46, 4-1/2-inch squares

Prairie Point Assembly

Step 1 Fold a 4-1/2-inch **ROSE #2** square in half diagonally, wrong sides together; press. Fold the triangle in half again; press.

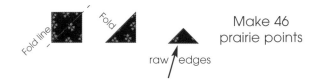

Make 46 prairie points

Step 2 Pin 5 prairie points to each short edge of the runner, overlapping them slightly. Adjust the prairie points to fit and hand baste them in place with a scant 1/4-inch seam allowance. The remaining prairie points will be added after the facing is sewn to the short ends.

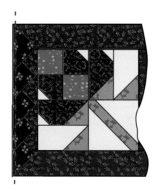

Facing

Cutting

From **ROSE PRINT #2**:
* Cut 3, 1-1/2 x 42-inch strips. Diagonally piece the strips as needed.
  From the strips cut:
  2, 1-1/2 x 44-inch facing strips
  2, 1-1/2 x 15-inch facing strips

Attaching the Facing

Step 1 With wrong sides together, fold each 1-1/2 x 15-inch **ROSE #2** facing strip in half lengthwise; press. With raw edges aligned, position the folded strips on the short edges of the runner, on top of the prairie points. Stitch the facing in place with a 1/4-inch seam allowance.

Step 2 Trim the excess facing even with the runner edge. Fold the facing to the back of the runner and hand stitch in place. <u>At this point the prairie points will lay out flat.</u>

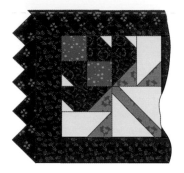

Step 3 Pin 18 prairie points to each long edge of the runner, overlapping them slightly and <u>extending the end prairie points 1/4-inch beyond the runner edges.</u> Adjust the prairie points to fit and hand baste them in place with a scant 1/4-inch seam allowance.

Step 4 With wrong sides together, fold each 44-inch long **ROSE #2** facing strip in half lengthwise; press. With raw edges aligned, position the folded strips on the long edges of the runner, on top of the prairie points. Stitch the facing in place with a 1/4-inch seam allowance. **Do not** trim the facing ends. Turn the excess facing under and fold the strip to the back of the runner so there will not be any raw edges showing; hand stitch in place. <u>At this point the prairie points will lay out flat.</u>

Summertime Prairie Point Runner
12 x 42-inches

ℬlossom Napkin Rings

Plain napkin rings become showy table accessories by simply gluing a large single artificial blossom to each ring.

Pumpkin Patchwork Napkins

16-inches square   Makes 4 napkins

Fabrics & Supplies
16, 6 x 20-inch pieces of **ASSORTED DARK PRINTS** for napkin tops
1 yard **GREEN PRINT** for napkin backs

Cutting
From **ASSORTED DARK PRINTS**:
• Cut 64, 4-1/2-inch squares

From **GREEN PRINT**:
• Cut 4, 16-1/2-inch squares

Piecing

Step 1 To make one napkin, use 16 of the 4-1/2-inch **DARK PRINT** squares. Sew the squares together in 4 rows of 4 squares each. Press the seam allowances in alternating directions by rows so the seams will fit snugly together with less bulk.

Step 2 Pin the rows at the block intersections, and sew the rows together. Press the seam allowances in one direction. <u>At this point the napkin top should measure 16-1/2-inches square.</u>

Step 3 With right sides together, layer the pieced napkin top and a 16-1/2-inch **GREEN** square. Sew the layers together 1/4-inch from the raw edges, leaving a 3-inch opening on one side for turning.

Step 4 Clip the corner seam allowances, turn the napkin right side out and press, taking care to see that the edges are sharp and even. Hand stitch the opening closed. Machine stitch in the ditch along the seam lines of the pieced napkin top.

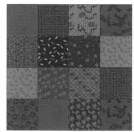

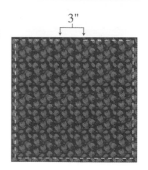

3"

Apple Harvest

Septembe

Apple Harvest

24 x 52-inches

Fabrics and Supplies

1/3 yard **RED PRINT#1** for apples,
pinwheel, and sawtooth units

1/4 yard **RED PRINT#2** for apples

1/4 yard **RED PLAID** for apples

3/8 yard **BEIGE PRINT** for background

6-inch square **BROWN PRINT** for apple stems

1/4 yard **DARK GREEN PRINT** for leaves
and center block

1/2 yard **MEDIUM GREEN PRINT** for
center block and lattice/inner border strips

5/8 yard **BLACK APPLE PRINT** for outer border

1/2 yard **RED PLAID** for binding (cut on the bias)

1-5/8 yards backing fabric

quilt batting, at least 28 x 56-inches

Before beginning this project, read through
Getting Started on page 77.

Apple/Leaf Blocks

Makes 2 blocks

Cutting

From **RED PRINT #1**:
- Cut 2, 5-1/2 x 6-1/2-inch rectangles

From **RED PRINT #2**:
- Cut 2, 5-1/2 x 6-1/2-inch rectangles

From **RED PLAID**:
- Cut 2, 5-1/2 x 6-1/2-inch rectangles

From **BEIGE PRINT**:
- Cut 1, 2-7/8 x 42-Inch strlp. From the strip cut:
  2, 2-7/8-inch squares
  2, 2-5/8-inch squares.
  Cut the squares in half diagonally to
  make 4 triangles.
  4, 2-1/2-inch squares
- Cut 2, 1-1/2 x 42-inch strips. From the strips cut:
  6, 1-1/2 x 4-1/2-inch rectangles
  6, 1-1/2 x 2-1/2-inch rectangles
  24, 1-1/2-inch squares

From **BROWN PRINT**:
- Cut 6, 1-1/2-inch squares

From **DARK GREEN PRINT**:
- Cut 1, 2-7/8 x 42-inch strip. From the strip cut:
  2, 2-7/8-inch squares. Trim the remaining strip
  to 2-1/2-inches wide and cut:
  2, 2-1/2 x 6-1/2-inch rectangles
  2, 2-1/2 x 4-1/2-inch rectangles
  2, 2-1/2-inch squares
  2, 1 x 5-inch stem strips

Piecing

Step 1 Position 1-1/2-inch **BEIGE** squares on the corners of a 5-1/2 x 6-1/2-inch **RED #1** rectangle. Draw diagonal lines on the squares and stitch on the lines. Trim the seam allowances to 1/4-inch; press. Repeat this process using the remaining **RED #1**, **RED #2**, and **RED PLAID** rectangles.

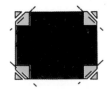

Make 2 RED #1
Make 2 RED #2
Make 2 RED PLAID

Step 2 Position a 1-1/2-inch **BROWN** square on the right corner of a 1-1/2 x 4-1/2-inch **BEIGE** rectangle. Draw a diagonal line on the square; stitch, trim, and press. Make 6 units. Sew a 1-1/2 x 2-1/2-inch **BEIGE** rectangle to the right edge of each unit. At this point each stem unit should measure 1-1/2 x 6-1/2-inches.

Make 6

Step 3 Sew the stem units to the top edge of each Step 1 unit. At this point each apple unit should measure 6-1/2-inches square.

Make 2 RED #1
Make 2 RED #2
Make 2 RED PLAID

Step 4 Position a 2-1/2-inch **BEIGE** square on the right corner of a **DARK GREEN** 2-1/2 x 4-1/2-inch rectangle. Draw a diagonal line on the square; stitch, trim, and press.

Make 2

Step 5 To make a leaf stem unit, center a **BEIGE** triangle on a 1 x 5-inch **DARK GREEN** strip; stitch together with a 1/4-inch seam allowance. Center another **BEIGE** triangle on the opposite edge of the **DARK GREEN** strip; stitch. Press the seam allowances toward the **DARK GREEN** strip. Trim the stem unit so it measures 2-1/2-inches square. Make 2 stem units. Sew the stem units to the left edge of the Step 4 units; press. At this point each leaf sub-unit should measure 2-1/2 x 6-1/2-inches.

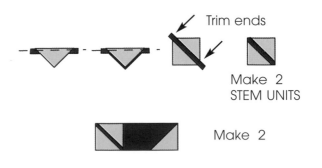

Trim ends

Make 2
STEM UNITS

Make 2

Step 6 Position a 2-1/2-inch **BEIGE** square on the right corner of a 2-1/2 x 6-1/2-inch **DARK GREEN** rectangle. Draw a diagonal line on the square; stitch, trim, and press.

 Make 2

Step 7 With right sides together, layer the 2-7/8-inch **DARK GREEN** and **BEIGE** squares together in pairs. Press together, but do not sew. Cut the layered squares in half diagonally to make 4 sets of triangles. Stitch 1/4-inch from the diagonal edge of each pair of triangles; press. Make 4 triangle-pieced squares. Sew the triangle-pieced squares together in pairs and sew a 2-1/2-inch **DARK GREEN** square to the right edge of each unit; press. At this point each leaf sub-unit should measure 2-1/2 x 6-1/2-inches.

Make 4, 2-1/2-inch triangle-pieced squares   Make 2

Step 8 Lay out the leaf sub-units; sew together and press. At this point each leaf unit should measure 6-1/2-inches square.

Make 2

Step 9 Refer to the block diagram for placement and sew together the leaf units and apple units; press. At this point each block should measure 12-1/2-inches square.

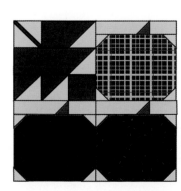

Make 2

Center Block

Cutting

From **RED PRINT #1**:
- Cut 1, 2-7/8 x 42-inch strip

From **BEIGE PRINT**:
- Cut 1, 2-7/8 x 42-inch strip

From **MEDIUM GREEN PRINT**:
- Cut 1, 2-1/2 x 42-inch strip. From the strip cut: 4, 2-1/2 x 4-1/2-inch rectangles

From **DARK GREEN PRINT**:
- Cut 1, 2-1/2 x 42-inch strip. From the strip cut: 8, 2-1/2-inch squares

Piecing

Step 1 With right sides together, layer the 2-7/8 x 42-inch **BEIGE** and **RED #1** strips. Press together, but do not sew. Cut the layered strip into squares. Cut each layered square in half diagonally to make 20 sets of triangles. Stitch 1/4-inch from the diagonal edge of each pair of triangles; press. At this point each triangle-pieced square should measure 2-1/2-inches square.

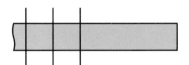

Crosscut 10, 2-7/8-inch squares

Make 20, 2-1/2-inch triangle-pieced squares

Step 2 To make the center pinwheel unit on page 54, sew together 4 triangle-pieced squares; press. Sew 2 of the 2-1/2 x 4-1/2-inch **MEDIUM GREEN** rectangles to the top/bottom edges of the pinwheel unit; press. Sew 2-1/2-inch **DARK GREEN** squares to both ends of the remaining **MEDIUM GREEN** rectangles; press. Sew the units to the side edges of the pinwheel unit; press. At this point the pinwheel unit should measure 8-1/2-inches square.

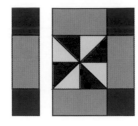

Make 1

Step 3 To make the sawtooth units, sew together 4 of the triangle-pieced squares; press. Make 4 sawtooth units. Sew 2 of the sawtooth units to the top/bottom edges of the pinwheel unit; press. Sew 2-1/2-inch **DARK GREEN** squares to both ends of the remaining sawtooth units; press. Sew the sawtooth units to the side edges of the pinwheel unit; press. At this point the center block should measure 12-1/2-inches square.

 Make 4

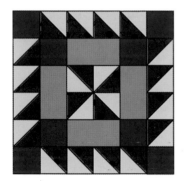 Make 1

Quilt Center and Borders

*Note: The yardage given allows for the border strips to be cut on the crosswise grain. Diagonally piece the strips as needed, referring to **Diagonal Piecing** instructions on page 80. Read through **Border** instructions on page 79 for general instructions on adding borders.*

Cutting

From **MEDIUM GREEN PRINT**:
- Cut 5, 2-1/2 x 42-inch strips. From the strips cut: 4, 2-1/2 x 12-1/2-inch lattice/inner border strips. The remaining strips will be used for side inner border strips.

From **BLACK APPLE PRINT**:
- Cut 4, 4-1/2 x 42-inch outer border strips

Quilt Center Assembly and Attaching the Borders

Step 1 Referring to the runner diagram for block placement, sew together the apple/leaf blocks, the center block, and the 4, 2-1/2 x 12-1/2-inch **MEDIUM GREEN** lattice/inner border strips; press.

Step 2 Attach the 2-1/2-inch wide **MEDIUM GREEN** side inner border strips.

Step 3 Attach the 4-1/2-inch wide **BLACK APPLE PRINT** outer border strips.

Putting It All Together

Trim the backing and batting so they are 4-inches larger than the runner top. Refer to **Finishing the Quilt** on page 80 for complete instructions.

Binding

Cutting

From **RED PLAID**:
- Cut enough 2-3/4-inch wide **bias** strips to make a 165-inch long strip

Sew the binding to the quilt using a 3/8-inch seam allowance. This measurement will produce a 1/2-inch wide finished double binding. Refer to **Binding** and **Diagonal Piecing** on page 80 for complete instructions.

Apple Harvest
24 x 52-inches

Treat Cups

Treat Cup pattern found on page 61

• To make a pattern for the cup covering, cut a paper cup apart at the seam and discard the bottom circle. Lay the cup pattern out flat. We used a 9 oz. Dixie Cold Cup for our project.

• Trace the cup pattern onto fusible web adding 1/4-inch at both side edges and at the bottom edge. Following the manufacturer's instructions, press the fusible web to the wrong side of Print fabric. Cut out the shape on the traced lines; peel off the paper backing. Fold the bottom edge up 1/4-inch; press.

• Fuse the fabric shape to a paper cup; overlap the back edges. Punch 2 handle attachment holes in the upper edge of the cup with an 1/8-inch paper punch.

• To make the handle, cut a 12-inch length of 18 gauge cloth covered stem wire. Paint the stem wire with gold metallic paint. While the paint is still wet, roll the stem wire in extra fine gold glitter; let dry. Shape the handle, turn up attachment loops at the ends. Insert the loops into the attachment holes; pinch tight with pliers.

• Cut a 26-inch length of 2-inch wide bias Plaid. Run a gathering stitch down the center of the fabric strip. Pull up the stitches, gathering the strip to fit around the top edge of the cup. Use Therm O Web Peel n Stick double sided adhesive to attach the gathered strip to the top edge of the cup; overlap the ends.

Pumpkin Glow

October

Pumpkin Glow

16 x 40-inches
Block: 4-inches square

Fabrics and Supplies

1/4 yard **BLACK PRINT** for center squares
and inner border

1/8 yard *each* of **7 ASSORTED DARK PRINTS**
for Log Cabin blocks

3/8 yard **ORANGE PUMPKIN PRINT** for outer border

1/8 yard **ORANGE FLORAL** for large pumpkin appliqués

1/8 yard **GOLD PRINT** for small pumpkin appliqués

5 x 9-inch piece **GREEN PRINT** for stem appliqués

3/8 yard **GREEN PLAID** for binding (cut on the bias)

1-1/4 yards backing fabric

quilt batting, at least 20 x 44-inches

paper-backed fusible web

machine-embroidery thread or pearl cotton: black

tear-away fabric stabilizer (optional)

*Before beginning this project, read through
Getting Started on page 77.*

Log Cabin Blocks

Makes 16 blocks

Cutting

From **BLACK PRINT**:
- Cut 1, 1-1/2 x 42-inch strip. From the strip cut: 16, 1-1/2-Inch center squares

From *each* of **7 ASSORTED DARK PRINTS**:
- Cut 3, 1 x 42-inch strips

Piecing

Note: Vary the position of the **ASSORTED DARK PRINT** fabrics from block to block to get a scrappy look. Follow Steps 1 through 3 to piece each of the 16 Log Cabin blocks.

Step 1 Sew a 1-inch wide **DARK PRINT** strip to a 1-1/2-inch **BLACK** center square. Press the seam allowance toward the strip. Trim the strip even with the edges of the center square creating a 2-piece unit.

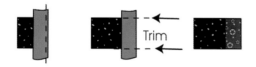

Step 2 Turn the unit a quarter turn to the left and stitch a different 1-inch wide **DARK PRINT** strip to the unit; press and trim.

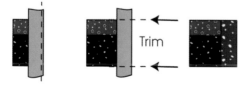

Step 3 Referring to the block diagram, continue adding the 1-inch wide **DARK PRINT** strips to complete the Log Cabin block. Press and trim each strip before adding the next. Each Log Cabin block should measure 4-1/2-inches square.

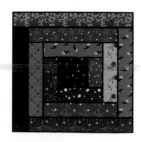

Mako 16

Step 4 Referring to the runner diagram, sew together the Log Cabin blocks in 2 rows of 8 blocks each. Press the seam allowances in alternating directions by rows so the seams will fit snugly together with less bulk. Sew the block rows together to make the quilt center; press. At this point the quilt center should measure 8-1/2 x 32-1/2-inches.

Borders

Note: The yardage given allows for the border strips to be cut on the crosswise grain. Read through **Border** instructions on page 79 for general instructions on adding borders.

Cutting

From **BLACK PRINT**:
- Cut 3, 1-1/2 x 42-inch inner border strips

From **ORANGE PUMPKIN PRINT**:
- Cut 3, 3-1/2 x 42-inch outer border strips

Attaching the Borders

Step 1 Attach the 1-1/2-inch wide **BLACK** inner border strips.

Step 2 Attach the 3-1/2-inch wide **ORANGE PUMPKIN PRINT** outer border strips.

Appliqué - Fusible Web Method

Step 1 Position the fusible web, paper side up, over the appliqué shapes. With a pencil, trace the shapes onto fusible web the number of times indicated on the pattern pieces, leaving a small margin between each shape. Cut the shapes apart.

Note: When you are fusing a large shape, like the pumpkin, fuse just the outer edges of the shape so that it will not look stiff when finished. To do this, draw a line about 3/8-inch inside the pumpkin, and cut away the fusible web on this line. Refer to page 78 in the **General Instructions** for a generic diagram of this technique. Shapes will vary depending on quilt design.

Step 2 Following the manufacturer's instructions, fuse the shapes to the wrong side of the fabric chosen for the appliqués. Let the fabric cool and cut along the traced line. Peel away the paper backing from the fusible web.

Step 3 Referring to the runner diagram, position the shapes on the runner top; fuse in place.

Note: We suggest pinning a rectangle of tear-away stabilizer to the backside of the runner top so that it will lay flat when the appliqué is complete. We use the extra-lightweight Easy Tear™ sheets as a stabilizer. When the appliqué is complete, tear away the stabilizer.

Step 4 We machine blanket stitched around the shapes using black Mettler® embroidery thread for the top thread and regular sewing thread in the bobbin. If you like, you could hand blanket stitch around the shapes with pearl cotton.

Blanket Stitch

Note: To prevent the hand blanket stitches from "rolling off" the edges of the appliqué shapes, take an extra backstitch in the same place as you made the blanket stitch, going around the outer curves, corners, and points. For straight edges, taking a backstitch every inch is enough.

Putting It All Together

Trim the backing and batting so they are 4-inches larger than the runner top. Refer to **Finishing the Quilt** on page 80 for complete instructions.

Binding

Cutting

From **GREEN PLAID**:
• Cut enough 2-3/4-inch wide **bias** strips to make a 130-inch long strip

Sew the binding to the quilt using a 3/8-inch seam allowance. This measurement will produce a 1/2-inch wide finished double binding. Refer to **Binding** and **Diagonal Piecing** on page 80 for complete instructions.

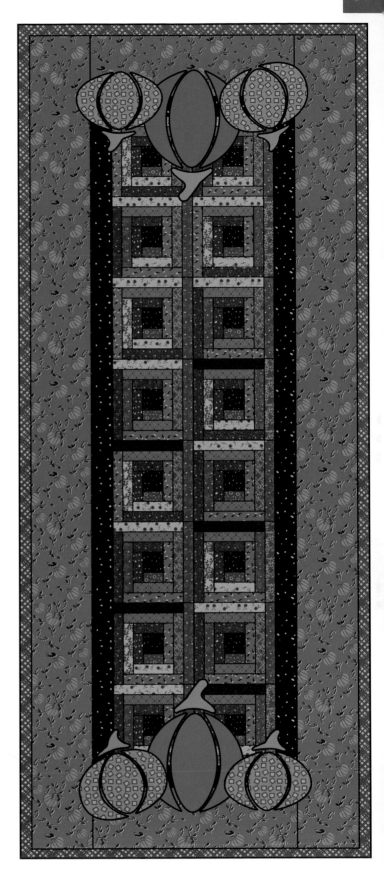

Pumpkin Glow
16 x 40-inches

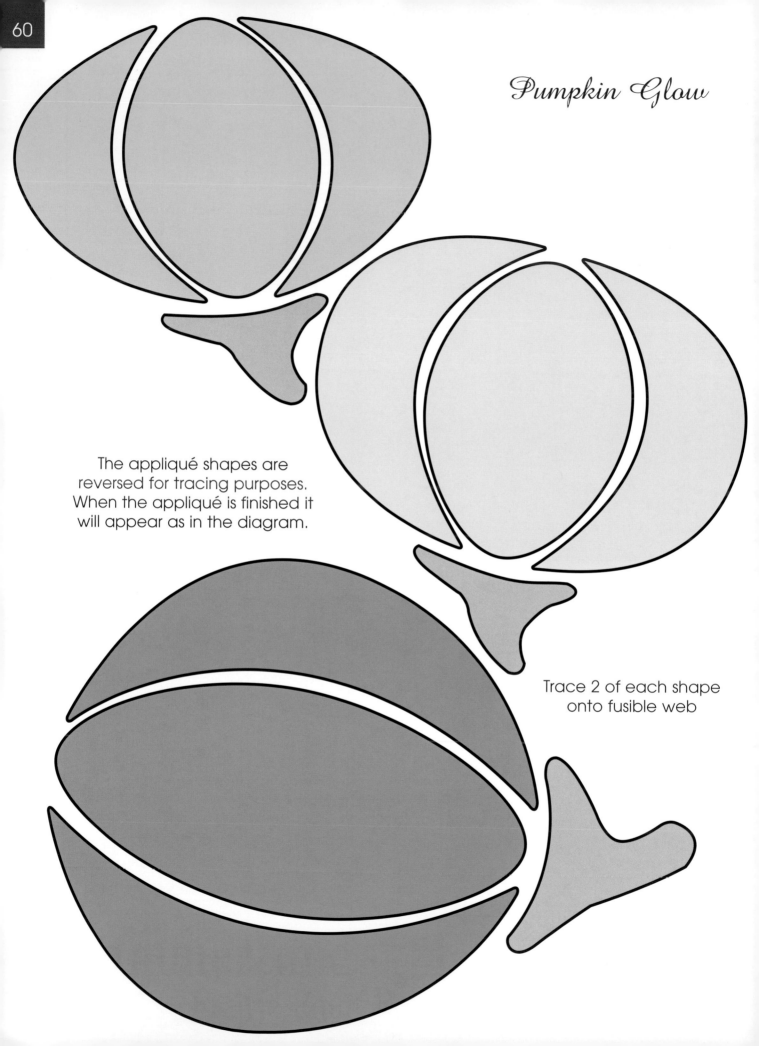

Pumpkin Glow

The appliqué shapes are reversed for tracing purposes. When the appliqué is finished it will appear as in the diagram.

Trace 2 of each shape onto fusible web

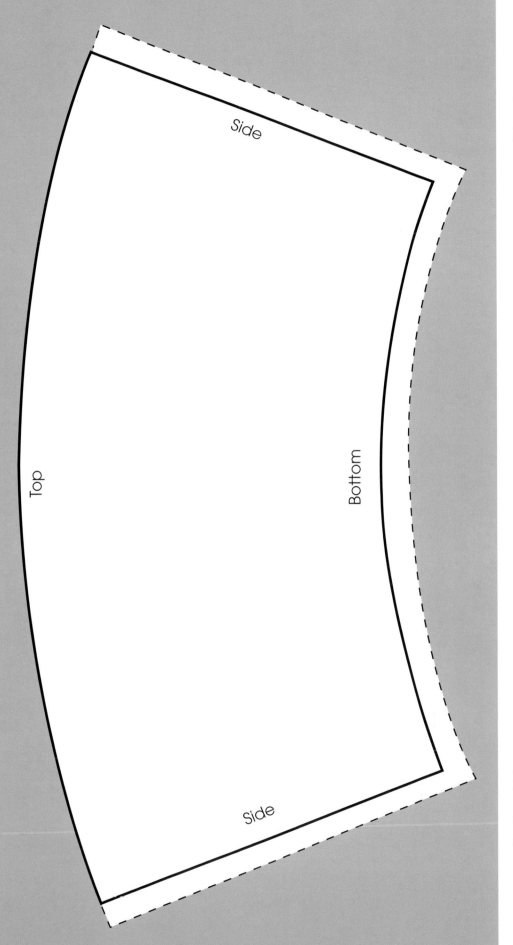

Side

Top

Bottom

Side

Treat Cups Pattern

Instructions on page 55

Supplies for craft projects in this book can be found at craft stores and/or floral shops.

Thank Your Lucky Stars

November

Thank Your Lucky Stars

16-1/2 x 22-1/2-inches

Fabrics and Supplies

5/8 yard **CREAM WOOL** for background, backing,
and circle border shapes

9 x 15-inch piece **GOLD WOOL** for stars

6-inch square **RED WOOL** for circle border shapes

13-inch square **BROWN WOOL** for circle border shapes

1/2 yard **TAN/RUST PLAID** for binding (cut on the bias)

paper-backed fusible web

No. 8 pearl cotton for decorative stitches: gold

freezer paper for appliqués

template material (template plastic or cardstock)

small, sharp scissors

No. 7 embroidery needle

3/4-inch sequin pins (optional), fabric glue (optional)

*Before beginning this project, read through
Getting Started on page 77.*

ALL WOOL SHOULD BE FELTED

• Felting wool (washing and drying) softens the fabric and interlocks the fibers. The felted wool is much less likely to ravel and it is perfect for making this project.

Tip: Do not mix wool colors during the felting process.

FELTING BY HAND (for smaller pieces):
• Boil the wool for 5 minutes, using a few drops

of detergent in the water. Squeeze out all excess moisture. Machine-dry the wool with a bath towel and a moderately high temperature. Press if necessary.

FELTING BY MACHINE (for larger pieces):
• Run the wool through the gentle wash cycle with hot water and a small amount of detergent (1 teaspoon). Machine-dry the wool with a bath towel and a moderately high temperature. Press if necessary.

Runner Top

Cutting

From **CREAM WOOL**:
• Cut 2, 12-1/4 x 18-inch background and backing rectangles

From **TAN/RUST PLAID**:
• Cut 1, 16-inch square; set aside.
• Cut enough 3-1/2-inch wide **bias** strips to make a 135-inch long binding strip

From Fusible Web:
• Cut 1, 16-inch square

Prepare the Background

Step 1 Referring to the diagram for measurements, divide one of the 12-1/4 x 18-inch **CREAM** background rectangles into 6 sections. Mark the placement lines lightly with a No. 2 lead pencil.

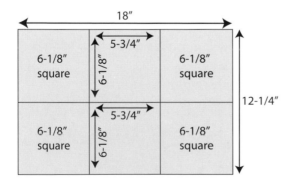

Step 2 Following the manufacturer's instructions, fuse the 16-inch fusible web square to the wrong side of the 16-inch **TAN/RUST PLAID** square.

From the **TAN/RUST PLAID** fused square:
• Cut 1, 1/2 x 20-inch **bias** strip
• Cut 2, 1/2 x 13-inch **bias** strips

Step 3 Using the placement lines as a guide, position the 13-inch long **bias** strips on the cream background rectangle; fuse in place. We machine feather stitched the strips in place using regular gold sewing thread. If you like, you could feather stitch the edges with pearl cotton. Position the 20-inch long **bias** strip on the cream background rectangle; fuse and stitch in place. Trim the ends as needed.

Feather Stitch

Step 4 Referring to **Basics for *Penny Woollies*™** and **PREPARING APPLIQUÉ SHAPES** prepare and stitch the stars on page 66 in place.

Basics for *Penny Woollies*™

Accurate tracing and cutting are the keys to your success.

Making Accurate Multiples of the Same Shape: (Stars and Circles)

Using a template is much faster and more accurate than tracing the shapes freehand.

• Trace the shape onto paper and cut out.
• Carefully trace the shape onto template material to make a template.
• Cut out the template on the line and trace the shape onto the dull side of the freezer paper.

Stitching Appliqués

• Use pearl cotton, embroidery needle, and blanket stitch to appliqué the shapes.
• Work with a long enough length of thread to eliminate the need to start a new thread.

Blanket Stitch

Preparing Appliqué Shapes

With a pencil, trace the shapes onto the dull side of the freezer paper. Trace the shapes the number of times indicated and allow at least 1/4-inch between each shape. Cut the shapes apart, leaving a small margin beyond the drawn lines.

Press the shiny side of the freezer paper shapes onto the felted wool using a medium setting on your iron. Let the wool cool. Freezer paper releases easily so use a few pins to anchor the freezer paper securely to the wool on each appliqué shape. Cut carefully and directly on the traced line using a small, sharp scissors. It is important to cut accurately. Remove and discard the freezer paper. The circle border shapes that surround the outside edge of the project must be cut accurately for proper fit.

Tip: I recommend 3/4-inch sequin pins. They are less likely to catch your thread.

Attaching the Shapes to the Background

Tip: It is always wise to plan ahead by arranging all the shapes on the cream background before stitching.

Adjust the shapes as necessary to match the photo. Remove all the pieces except those you are stitching. Use pins or a small amount of fabric glue to secure the appliqué shapes in place. As you stitch, the appliqué shapes tend to shift. Pinning or gluing the appliqué shapes will keep them in place. Blanket stitch the shapes in place.

Binding

Step 1 Place the finished *Penny Woollie* top on the cream backing piece; baste the edges together.

Step 2 Diagonally piece the 3-1/2-inch wide **TAN/RUST PLAID** binding strips together. Fold the strip in half lengthwise, wrong sides together; press. Unfold and trim one end at a 45° angle. Turn under 1/4-inch; press. Refold the strip.

Step 3 With raw edges of the binding and *Penny Woollie* even, stitch with a 1/2-inch seam allowance. Refer to **Binding** and **Diagonal Piecing** on page 80 for complete instructions.

Circle Border

Step 1 Blanket stitch a small A brown circle to a medium B cream circle. Layer this shape on another medium B cream circle; blanket stitch the edges together. Make a total of 26 circle border shapes. (I used a 36-inch length of pearl cotton to eliminate starting a new thread.)

Step 2 Blanket stitch a medium C red circle to a large D cream circle. Layer this shape on another large D cream circle; blanket stitch the edges together. Make a total of 4 circle corner border shapes. (I used a 43-inch length of pearl cotton to eliminate starting a new thread.)

Step 3 To attach the circle border shapes, place the *Penny Woollie* center face down on a flat surface. Mark the midpoints of each side of the *Penny Woollie* to give you a guideline to accurately position the border shapes. Place the border shapes face down around the *Penny Woollie* center as diagramed.

Step 4 Place a pin connecting each border circle shape to the backing. Tack each circle to the *Penny Woollie* center backing with 4 small whip stitches and regular cream sewing thread. Be sure to keep the *Penny Woollie* flat while stitching and do not stitch through to the right side. Knot and bury the end of the thread by slipping your needle between the 2 layers of the *Penny Woollie*. Cut the thread close to the fabric.

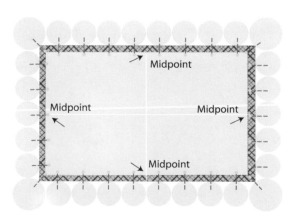

Step 5 Place a pin to connect each of the circle border shapes at the point at which their edges touch going around the *Penny Woollie* center. Tack the shapes together at this point with 4 small whip stitches and regular cream sewing thread. Keep the *Penny Woollie* flat while stitching and do not stitch through to the right side. Knot, bury, and cut the thread.

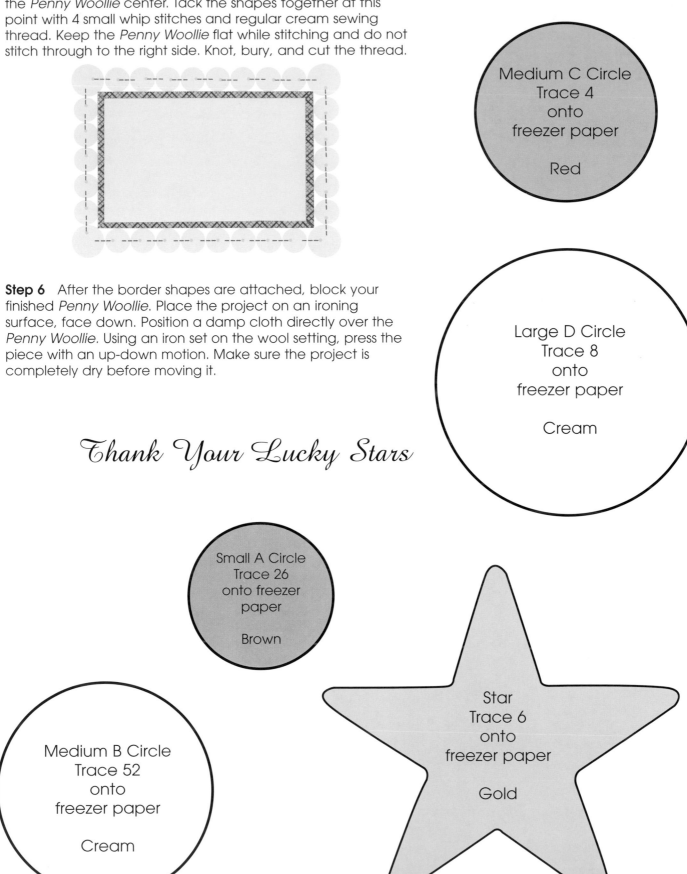

Medium C Circle
Trace 4
onto
freezer paper

Red

Step 6 After the border shapes are attached, block your finished *Penny Woollie*. Place the project on an ironing surface, face down. Position a damp cloth directly over the *Penny Woollie*. Using an iron set on the wool setting, press the piece with an up-down motion. Make sure the project is completely dry before moving it.

Thank Your Lucky Stars

Large D Circle
Trace 8
onto
freezer paper

Cream

Small A Circle
Trace 26
onto freezer
paper

Brown

Medium B Circle
Trace 52
onto
freezer paper

Cream

Star
Trace 6
onto
freezer paper

Gold

Thanksgiving Favors

These pumpkin pots serve well as individual place setting favors
or as decorative accessories throughout the house.
Place a small decorative candle ring on a 3-1/2" clay pot.
Rest a small artificial pumpkin in the center of the candle ring.

$\mathcal{P}$oinsettia Penny Woollie™
& Holly Sprig Runner

December

Poinsettia Penny Woollie™
& Holly Sprig Runner

Fabrics and Supplies
for Holly Sprig Runner
21 x 39-inches

5/8 yard **RED FLORAL** for runner center rectangle

1/8 yard **GOLD PRINT** for inner bands

1/4 yard **ROSE PRINT** for outer bands

9-inch square **GREEN WOOL** for holly leaf appliqués

5-inch square **RED WOOL** for holly berry appliqués

1/2 yard **GREEN PLAID** for binding (cut on the bias)

3/4 yard backing fabric

quilt batting, at least 25 x 43-inches

No. 8 pearl cotton for decorative stitches: gold

freezer paper for appliqués

small, sharp scissors

No. 7 embroidery needle

3/4-inch sequin pins (optional)

fabric glue (optional)

*Before beginning this project, read through
Getting Started on page 77.*

Holly Sprig Runner

21 x 39-inches

Cutting

From **RED FLORAL** :
- Cut 1, 21 x 42-inch strip. From the strip cut:
  1, 21 x 24-1/2-inch runner center rectangle

From **GOLD PRINT**:
- Cut 1, 2 x 42-inch strip. From the strip cut:
  2, 2 x 21-inch strips

From **ROSE PRINT**:
- Cut 1, 6-1/2 x 42-inch strip. From the strip cut:
  2, 6-1/2 x 21-inch strips

Piecing

Step 1 Referring to the runner diagram, sew the 2-inch wide **GOLD** strips and the 6-1/2-inch wide **ROSE** strips to both side edges of the 21 x 24-1/2-inch **RED FLORAL** runner center rectangle; press. At this point the runner should measure 21 x 39-1/2-inches.

Step 2 Referring to **Basics for *Penny Woollies*** and **PREPARING APPLIQUÉ SHAPES** on page 71, prepare and stitch the leaves and berries in place.

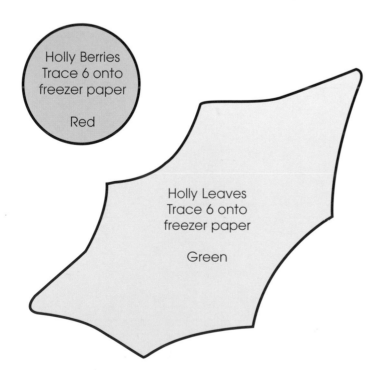

Holly Berries
Trace 6 onto
freezer paper

Red

Holly Leaves
Trace 6 onto
freezer paper

Green

Putting It All Together

Trim the backing and batting so they are 4-inches larger than the runner top. Refer to **Finishing the Quilt** on page 80 for complete instructions.

Binding

Cutting

From **GREEN PLAID**:
- Cut enough 2-3/4-inch wide **bias** strips to make a 130-inch long strip

Sew the binding to the runner using a 3/8-inch seam allowance. This measurement will produce a 1/2-inch wide finished double binding. Refer to **Binding** and **Diagonal Piecing** in page 80 for complete instructions.

Holly Sprig Runner
21 x 39-inches

Fabrics and Supplies
for Poinsettia Penny Woollie™
18-1/2 x 21-inches

22 x 56-inch piece **CREAM WOOL** for background, backing, and circle border shapes

9 x 33-inch piece **RED WOOL** for petals and circle border shapes

7 x 40-inch piece **GREEN WOOL** for leaves and circle border shapes

5-inch square **GOLD WOOL** for flower center circles

No. 8 pearl cotton for decorative stitches: gold

freezer paper for appliqués

template material (template plastic or cardstock)

small, sharp scissors

No. 7 embroidery needle

3/4-inch sequin pins (optional)

fabric glue (optional)

ALL WOOL SHOULD BE FELTED

- Felting wool (washing and drying) softens the fabric and interlocks the fibers. The felted wool is much less likely to ravel and it is perfect for making this project.

Tip: Do not mix wool colors during the felting process.

FELTING BY HAND (for smaller pieces):
- Boil the wool for 5 minutes, using a few drops of detergent in the water. Squeeze out all excess moisture. Machine-dry the wool with a bath towel and a moderately high temperature. Press if necessary.

FELTING BY MACHINE (for larger pieces):
- Run the wool through the gentle wash cycle with hot water and a small amount of detergent (1 teaspoon). Machine-dry the wool with a bath towel and a moderately high temperature. Press if necessary.

About our fabric requirements . . . extra yardage is allowed so the wool can be felted (prewashed). 100% wool can shrink up to 20% in width and length; wool blends less. To avoid future shrinkage upon completion of your *Penny Woollies* project, dry cleaning is recommended.

Poinsettia Penny Woollie™

Basics for *Penny Woollies*

Accurate tracing and cutting are the keys to your success.

Making Accurate Multiples of the Same Shape: (Circles)

Using a template is much faster and more accurate than tracing the shapes freehand.

- Trace the shape onto paper and cut out.
- Carefully trace the shape onto template material to make a template.
- Cut out the template on the line and trace the shape onto the dull side of the freezer paper.

Stitching Appliqués

- Use pearl cotton, embroidery needle, and blanket stitch to appliqué the shapes.
- Work with a long enough length of thread to eliminate the need to start a new thread.

Blanket Stitch

Preparing Appliqué Shapes

With a pencil, trace the shapes onto the dull side of the freezer paper. Trace the shapes the number of times indicated and allow at least 1/4-inch between each shape. Cut the shapes apart, leaving a small margin beyond the drawn lines.

Press the shiny side of the freezer paper shapes onto the felted wool using a medium setting on your iron. Let the wool cool. Freezer paper releases easily so use a few pins to anchor the freezer paper securely to the wool on each appliqué shape. Cut carefully and directly on the traced line using a small, sharp scissors. It is important to cut accurately. Remove and discard the freezer paper.

The circle border shapes that surround the outside edge of the **POINSETTIA** *Penny Woollie* must be cut accurately for proper fit.

Tip: I recommend 3/4-inch sequin pins. They are less likely to catch your thread.

Attaching the Shapes to the Background

Tip: It is always wise to plan ahead by arranging all the shapes on the cream background before stitching.

Adjust the shapes as necessary to match the photo and diagram on page 74. Remove all the pieces except those you are stitching. Use pins or a small amount of fabric glue to secure the appliqué shapes in place. As you stitch, the appliqué shapes tend to shift. Pinning or gluing the appliqué shapes will keep them in place. Blanket stitch the shapes in place.

Secure the flower center circles with a French knot in the center of each circle. Outline stitch the tendrils.

Place the finished *Penny Woollie* top on the cream backing piece; blanket stitch the edges together with pearl cotton.

French Knot Stitch

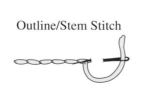
Outline/Stem Stitch

Circle Border

Step 1 Blanket stitch a small red or green circle to a large cream circle. Layer this shape on another large cream circle; blanket stitch the edges together. Make a total of 22 circle border shapes. (I used a 36-inch length of pearl cotton to eliminate starting a new thread.)

Step 2 To attach the circle border shapes, place the *Penny Woollie* center face down on a flat surface. Mark the midpoints of each side of the *Penny Woollie* to give you a guideline to accurately position the border shapes. Place the border shapes face down around the *Penny Woollie* center as diagramed.

Step 3 Place a pin connecting each border circle shape to the backing. Tack each circle to the *Penny Woollie* center backing with 4 small whip stitches and regular cream sewing thread. Be sure to keep the *Penny Woollie* flat while stitching and do not stitch through to the right side. Knot and bury the end of the thread by slipping your needle between the 2 layers of the *Penny Woollie*. Cut the thread close to the fabric.

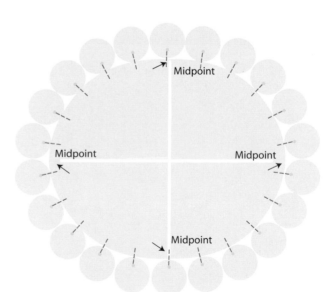

Step 4 Place a pin to connect each of the circle border shapes at the point at which their edges touch going around the *Penny Woollie* center. Tack the shapes together at this point with 4 small whip stitches and regular cream sewing thread. Keep the *Penny Woollie* flat while stitching and do not stitch through to the right side. Knot, bury, and cut the thread.

Step 5 After the border shapes are attached, block your finished *Penny Woollie*. Place the project on an ironing surface, face down. Position a damp cloth directly over the *Penny Woollie*. Using an iron set on the wool setting, press the piece with an up-down motion. Make sure the *Penny Woollie* is completely dry before moving it.

The appliqué shapes are <u>not</u> reversed for tracing purposes, because generally wool has no right or wrong side.

Poinsettia Penny Woollie™

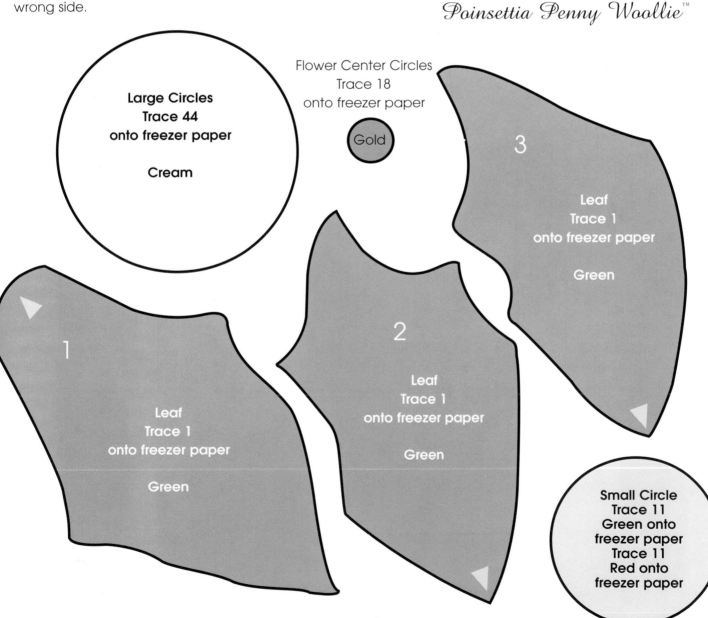

Large Circles
Trace 44
onto freezer paper

Cream

Flower Center Circles
Trace 18
onto freezer paper

Gold

3
Leaf
Trace 1
onto freezer paper

Green

1
Leaf
Trace 1
onto freezer paper

Green

2
Leaf
Trace 1
onto freezer paper

Green

Small Circle
Trace 11
Green onto
freezer paper
Trace 11
Red onto
freezer paper

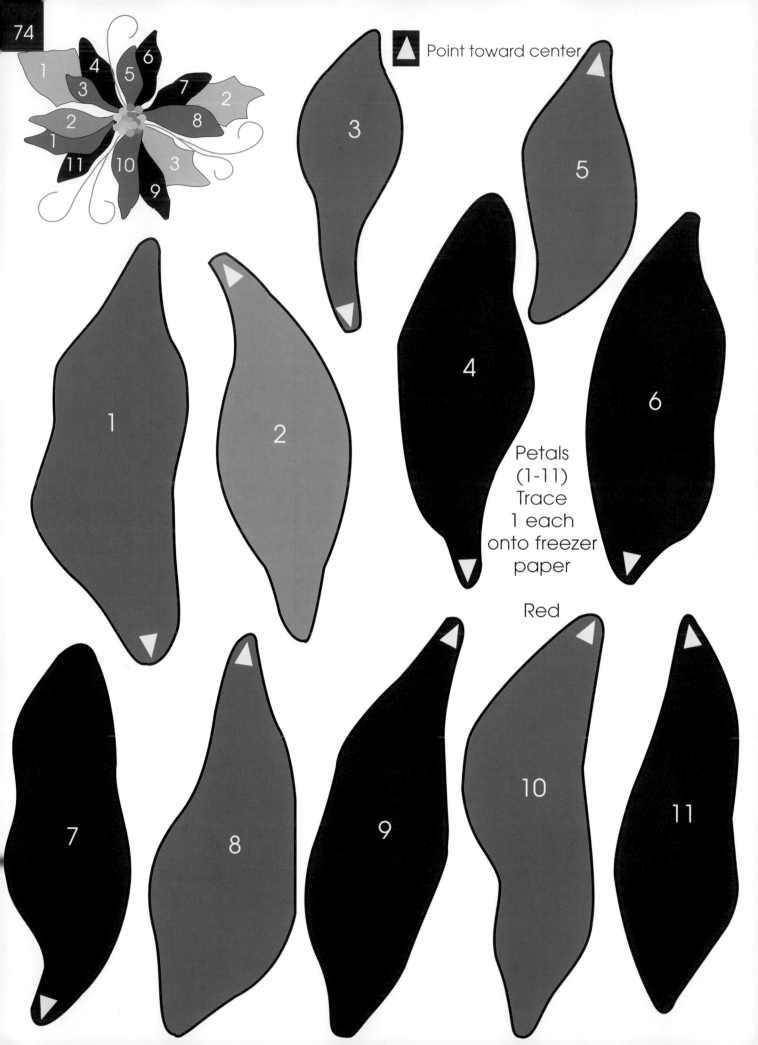

△ Point toward center

3

5

1

2

4

6

Petals
(1-11)
Trace
1 each
onto freezer
paper

Red

7

8

9

10

11

Poinsettia Penny Woollie™

1/4 of Background and Backing Oval

Trace 2 onto freezer paper

Cream

This shape represents a quarter of
the oval shape needed for the
Background/Backing Oval. Fold a
16 x 18-inch piece of freezer paper
in half and in half again. Place the
folds on the solid lines; trace
and cut out.

Evergreen & Berry "Bells"

Add sparkle to a holiday table setting with these
miniature evergreen and berry "bells."

- *Paint small terra cotta pots a creamy white. To add glitter to pots coat with slightly diluted white glue and roll in glitter.*

- *Invert pot and decorate with small sprigs of artificial evergreens and berries.*

General Instructions

Getting Started

Yardage is based on 42-inch wide fabric. If your fabric is wider or narrower it will affect the amount of necessary strips you need to cut in some patterns, and of course, it will affect the amount of fabric you have left over. Generally, THIMBLEBERRIES patterns allow for a little extra fabric so you can confidently cut your pattern pieces with ease.

A rotary cutter, mat, and wide clear plastic ruler with 1/8-inch markings are needed tools in attaining accuracy. A beginner needs good tools just as an experienced quilt maker needs good equipment. A 24 x 36-inch mat board is a good size to own. It will easily accommodate the average quilt fabrics and will aid in accurate cutting. The plastic ruler you purchase should be at least 6 x 24-inches and easy to read. Do not purchase a smaller ruler to save money, the large size will be invaluable to your quilt making success.

It is often recommended to prewash and press fabrics to test for color fastness and possible shrinkage. If you choose to prewash, wash in cool water and dry in a cool to moderate dryer. Industry standards actually suggest that line drying is best. Shrinkage is generally very minimal and usually is not a concern. A good way to test your fabric for both shrinkage and color fastness is to cut a 3-inch square of fabric. Soak the fabric in a white bowl filled with water. Squeeze the water out of the fabric and press it dry on a piece of muslin. If the fabric is going to release color it will do so either in the water or when it is pressed dry. Re-measure the 3-inch fabric square to see if it has changed size considerably (more than 1/4-inch). If it has, wash, dry, and press the entire yardage. This little test could save you hours in prewashing and pressing.

Read instructions thoroughly before beginning a project. Each step will make more sense to you when you have a general overview of the whole process. Take one step at time and follow the illustrations. They will often make more sense to you than the words. Take "baby steps" so you don't get overwhelmed by the entire process.

When working with flannel and other loosely woven fabrics, always prewash and dry. These fabrics almost always shrink some.

For piecing, place right sides of the fabric pieces together and use 1/4-inch seam allowances throughout the entire quilt unless otherwise specifically stated in the directions. An accurate seam allowance is the most important part of the quilt making process after accurate cutting. All the directions are based on accurate 1/4-inch seam allowances. It is very important to check your sewing machine to see what position your fabric should be to get accurate seams. To test, use a piece of 1/4-inch graph paper, stitch along the quarter inch line as if the paper were fabric. Make note of where the edge of the paper lines up with your presser foot or where it lines up on the throat plate of your machine. Many quilters place a piece of masking tape on the throat plate to help guide the edge of the fabric. Now test your seam allowance on fabric. Cut 2, 2-1/2-inch squares, place right sides together and stitch along one edge. Press seam allowances in one direction and measure. At this point the unit should measure 2-1/2 x 4-1/2-inches. If it does not, adjust your stitching guidelines and test again. Seam allowances are included in the cutting sizes given in this book.

Pressing is a very important step in quilt making. As a general rule, you should never cross a stitched seam with another seam unless it has been pressed. Therefore, every time you stitch a seam it needs to be pressed before adding another piece. Often, it will feel like you press as much as you sew, and often that is true. It is very important that you press and not iron the seams. Pressing is a firm, up and down motion that will flatten the seams but not distort the piecing. Ironing is a back and forth motion and will stretch and distort the small pieces. Most quilters use steam to help the pressing process. The moisture does help and will not distort the shapes as long as the pressing motion is used.

An old fashioned rule is to press seam allowances in one direction, toward the darker fabric. Often, background fabrics are light in color and pressing toward the darker fabric prevents the seam allowances from showing through to the right side. Pressing seam allowances in one direction is thought to create a stronger seam. Also, for ease in hand quilting, the quilting lines should fall on the side of the seam which is opposite the seam allowance. As you piece quilts, you will find these "rules" to be helpful but not necessarily always appropriate. Sometimes seams need to be pressed in the opposite direction so the seams of different units will fit together more easily which quilters refer to as seams "nesting" together. When sewing together two units with opposing seam allowances, use the tip of your seam ripper to gently guide the units under your presser foot. Sometimes it is necessary to re-press the seams to make the units fit together nicely. Always try to achieve the least bulk in one spot and accept that no matter which way you press, it may be a little tricky and it could be a little bulky.

Pressing direction

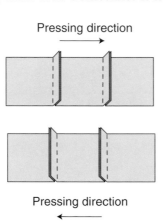

Pressing direction

Fusible Web Appliqué

Note: When you are fusing a large shape, fuse just the outer edges of the shape so that it will not look stiff when finished. To do this, draw a line about 3/8-inch inside the shape and cut away the fusible web on this line.

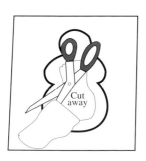

Cut away

Tools and Equipment

Making beautiful quilts does not require a large number of specialized tools or expensive equipment. My list of favorites is short and sweet, and includes the things I use over and over again because they are always accurate and dependable.

• I find a long acrylic ruler indispensable for accurate rotary cutting. The ones I like most are an Omnigrid 6 x 24-inch grid acrylic ruler for cutting long strips and squaring up fabrics and quilt tops, and a Master Piece® 45, 8 x 24-inch ruler for cutting 6- to 8-inch wide borders. I sometimes tape together two 6 x 24-inch acrylic rulers for cutting borders up to 12-inches wide.

• A 15-inch Omnigrid square acrylic ruler is great for squaring up individual blocks and corners of a quilt top, for cutting strips up to 15-inches wide or long, and for trimming side and corner triangles.

• I think the markings on my 24 x 36-inch Olfa rotary cutting mat stay visible longer than on other mats, and the lines are fine and accurate.

• The largest size Olfa rotary cutter cuts through many layers of fabric easily, and it isn't cumbersome to use. The 2-1/2-inch blade slices through three layers of backing, batting, and a quilt top like butter.

• An 8-inch pair of Gingher shears is great for cutting out appliqué templates and cutting fabric from a bolt or fabric scraps.

• I keep a pair of 5-1/4-inch Gingher scissors by my sewing machine, so it is handy for both machine work and handwork. This size is versatile and sharp enough to make large and small cuts equally well.

• My Grabbit® magnetic pin cushion has a surface that is large enough to hold lots of straight pins, and a strong magnet that keeps them securely in place.

• Silk pins are long and thin, which means they won't leave large holes in your fabric. I like them because they increase accuracy in pinning pieces or blocks together, and it is easy to press over silk pins, as well.

• For pressing individual pieces, blocks, and quilt tops, I use an 18 x 48-inch sheet of plywood covered with several layers of cotton fiberfill and topped with a layer of muslin stapled to the back. The 48-inch length allows me to press an entire width of fabric at one time without the need to reposition it, and the square ends are better than tapered ends on an ironing board for pressing finished quilt tops.

Rotary Cutting

• "Square off" the ends of your fabric before measuring and cutting pieces. This means that the cut edge of the fabric must be exactly perpendicular to the folded edge which creates a 90º angle. Align the folded and selvage edges of the fabric with the lines on the cutting board, and place a ruled square on the fold. Place a 6 x 24-inch ruler against the side of the square to get a 90º angle. Hold the ruler in place, remove the square, and cut along the edge of the ruler. If you are left-handed, work from the other end of the fabric. Use the lines on your cutting board to help line up fabric, but not to measure and cut strips. Use a ruler for accurate cutting, always checking to make sure your fabric is lined up with horizontal and vertical lines on the ruler.

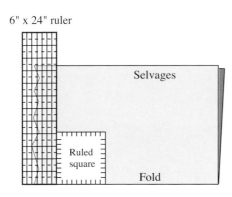

6" x 24" ruler
Selvages
Ruled square
Fold

Cutting Strips

• When cutting strips or rectangles, cut on the crosswise grain. Strips can then be cut into squares or smaller rectangles.

• If your strips are not straight after cutting a few of them, refold the fabric, align the folded and selvage edges with the lines on the cutting board, and "square off" the edge again by trimming to straighten, and begin cutting.

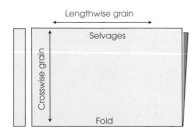

Lengthwise grain
Selvages
Crosswise grain
Fold

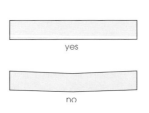

yes

no

Borders

Note: *Cut borders to the width called for. Always cut border strips a few inches longer than needed, just to be safe. Diagonally piece the border strips together as needed.*

Step 1 With pins, mark the center points along all 4 sides of the quilt. For the top and bottom borders measure the quilt from left to right through the middle.

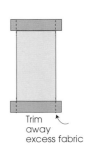

Step 2 Measure and mark the border lengths and center points on the strips cut for the borders before sewing them on.

Step 3 Pin the border strips to the quilt and stitch a 1/4-inch seam. Press the seam allowance toward the borders. Trim off excess border lengths.

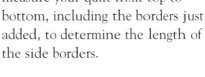

Step 4 For the side borders, measure your quilt from top to bottom, including the borders just added, to determine the length of the side borders.

Trim away excess fabric

Step 5 Measure and mark the side border lengths as you did for the top and bottom borders.

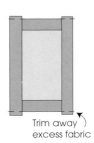

Step 6 Pin and stitch the side border strips in place. Press and trim the border strips even with the borders just added.

Trim away excess fabric

Step 7 If your quilt has multiple borders, measure, mark, and sew additional borders to the quilt in the same manner.

Finishing the Quilt

Step 1 Remove the selvages from the backing fabric. Sew the long edges together; press. Trim the backing and batting so they are 4-inches larger than the quilt top.

Step 2 Mark the quilt top for quilting. Layer the backing, batting, and quilt top. Baste the 3 layers together and quilt.

Step 3 When quilting is complete, remove basting. Baste all 3 layers together a scant 1/4-inch from the edge. This basting keeps the layers from shifting and prevents puckers from forming when adding the binding. Trim excess batting and backing fabric even with the edge of the quilt top. Add the binding as shown.

Diagonal Piecing

Stitch diagonally   Trim to 1/4" seam allowance   Press seam open

Binding

Step 1 Diagonally piece the binding strips. Fold the strip in half lengthwise, wrong sides together; press.

Double-Layer Binding

Step 2 Unfold and trim one end at a 45° angle. Turn under the edge 1/4-inch; press. Refold the strip.

Fold Line

Step 3 With raw edges of the binding and quilt top even, stitch with a 3/8-inch seam allowance, unless otherwise specified, starting 2-inches from the angled end.

Step 4 Miter the binding at the corners. As you approach a corner of the quilt, stop sewing 1/4 to 1-inch from the corner of the quilt (use the same measurement as your seam allowance).

1/4" to 1"
Binding Strip
Quilt Top

Step 5 Clip the threads and remove the quilt from under the presser foot.

Step 6 Flip the binding strip up and away from the quilt, then fold the binding down even with the raw edge of the quilt. Begin sewing at the upper edge. Miter all 4 corners in this manner.

Quilt Top   Quilt Top

Step 7 Trim the end of the binding so it can be tucked inside of the beginning binding about 1/2-inch. Finish stitching the seam.

Quilt Top   Quilt Top

Step 8 Turn the folded edge of the binding over the raw edges and to the back of the quilt so that the stitching line does not show. Hand sew the binding in place, folding in the mitered corners as you stitch.

Quilt Back   Quilt Back   Quilt Back